MOTHER CHRISTMAS

MOTHER CHRISTMAS

by David Lewis

JOSEF WEINBERGER PLAYS

LONDON

MOTHER CHRISTMAS
First published in 2017
by Josef Weinberger Ltd
12-14 Mortimer Street, London W1T 3JJ
www.josef-weinberger.com / plays@jwmail.co.uk

ISBN: 978 0 85676 367 0

Printed by Short Run Press Ltd, Exeter

MOTHER CHRISTMAS was first performed at the Hampstead Theatre Downstairs on 8th December 2017. The cast was as follows:

MAGGIE	Diana Quick
DAVINA	Alexandra Gilbreath
BEN	Jamie Ballard
GRACE	Ritu Arya
PETER	Joseph Mydell

Directed by Donnacadh O'Briain
Designed by Sarah Beaton
Lighting design by Oliver Fenwick
Sound design by John Leonard
Assistant director Octavia Gilmore
Stage Manager Sarah Barnes

CHARACTERS

Maggie. 72. Mother of Davina and Ben.

Davina. 49. Daughter of Maggie, mother of Grace.

Ben. 45. Son of Maggie, brother of Davina.

Grace. 22. Daughter of Davina.

Peter. 67. Retired GP.

A Christmas family gathering. A reception room in MAGGIE'S *home. Some Christmas decorations including a Christmas tree. Lots of presents under the tree.*

There are two exits. One, without door, leads to the kitchen (or kitchen/diner) and the back door of the house. (The kitchen may be partially visible.) The other exit, through the only visible door, leads to the remainder of the house. Required furniture includes sofa and armchair. There is an iPod dock but no television as this lives in a second reception room.

Three acts (interval after act two) are set over three consecutive Christmas Eves.

ACT ONE

Scene One

GRACE, *wearing a penguin onesie, is taking selfies in front of the Christmas tree. (*GRACE *is pregnant but in the early stages, nothing noticeable.) The fairy lights flicker and go out. She investigates.*

A timer alarm is heard from the kitchen. A few moments later, DAVINA *enters as a glamorous Mother Christmas and walks swiftly into the room . . .*

DAVINA   That's my pies.

        (*. . . and out into the kitchen.* MAGGIE *enters as the Virgin Mary.*)

MAGGIE   I don't see why we need mince pies. There's so much food.

GRACE   The lights aren't working.

        (*She shuffles out to the kitchen, playing with her iPhone.* MAGGIE *frowns, then examines the fairy lights while softly singing 'Have Yourself a Merry Little Christmas' to herself.* DAVINA *enters.*)

DAVINA   What's the matter?

MAGGIE   The blasted lights are off again.

        (MAGGIE *exits to the kitchen.*)

DAVINA   Oh, no.

        (BEN *enters in a ridiculous oven-ready turkey costume. He is not happy.*)

BEN   This is not comfortable.

DAVINA   No. I'm sure. Where did you get it?

BEN	That party shop. In the High Street. It's all they had.
DAVINA	Seriously?
BEN	The last turkey in the shop.
DAVINA	They didn't have a Santa costume?
BEN	Yes, but too small.
DAVINA	Really?
BEN	Way too small. Would have looked ridiculous.

(DAVINA *stares at him for a moment then begins tidying the room, making it as presentable as possible.*)

DAVINA	God forbid you look ridiculous . . .
BEN	Anyway, there's bound to be Santas. We don't want too many Santas, do we?
DAVINA	I don't know why you leave everything to the last minute.
BEN	I don't. I've just been . . . really busy, recently.
DAVINA	(*beat*) Have you? That's good.
BEN	(*sensing her doubt*) Yes, I have.
DAVINA	I saw your new website. Very professional.
BEN	(*beat*) It is a profession.
DAVINA	(*beat*) Yes. I know. I'm saying it was very good. Why is it so hard to give you compliments?
BEN	Last year, you said I should think about a career. As if gardening isn't a career.

DAVINA   Let's forget about last Christmas, shall we? I'm sure we all said things we regret.

              (DAVINA *finds her handbag, takes some pills out of it and puts them in her pocket. Then she continues tidying.*)

BEN   You still taking the Prozac?

              (*She looks at him.*)

DAVINA   Yes, but these are my Christmas pills. Propranolol. Anti-anxiety. I just like having some on me in case I need them. (*Beat.*) I'm a bit worried about Mum's Virgin Mary costume. Nigel and Val are very Catholic.

BEN   How many are coming?

DAVINA   Um . . . Twentyish.

BEN   Are we sure Dad is up to this?

DAVINA   Dad's not coming. (BEN *stares, shocked.*) He's too weak. We're picking him up tomorrow, after lunch, hopefully.

BEN   Are you serious?

DAVINA   Ben, he's very ill.

BEN   Then, why are we having the party? I thought this was for Dad.

DAVINA   Yes. Partly. It's a bit late to cancel.

BEN   I thought the only reason we're doing this is because it's . . .

              (*Pause. They stare.*)

DAVINA   It's what? Dad's last Christmas?

BEN   Well, we're all aware of that, aren't we? How ill is
              he, exactly?

DAVINA   Not sure. Mum wouldn't let me go with her this
              morning.

BEN   You don't need her permission.

DAVINA   No. Well, I thought I'd see him tonight. So, I didn't
              argue.

BEN   He's not . . . on the way out?

DAVINA   No. No. No, I don't think so. He's just had a bad
              couple of days.

              (MAGGIE *enters with a glass of sherry.*)

MAGGIE   Ben, the fairy lights aren't working.

BEN   So, Dad's missing the party.

MAGGIE   Sorry?

BEN   Dad. Davina says he's not well enough.

MAGGIE   We'll pick him up tomorrow. The fairy lights aren't
              working. Please will you take a look?

BEN   We're not cancelling?

MAGGIE   Cancelling? Cancelling what? Christmas?

BEN   The party.

DAVINA   Mummy, that's a Virgin Mary costume, is it?

MAGGIE   Um . . . No, I think it's just . . . generically biblical.

DAVINA   Really?

              (MAGGIE *looks at her.*)

MAGGIE	Why? What's the matter? (*Beat.*) We look like the Madonna and the whore, do we? (DAVINA *stares.*) I'm only joking.
DAVINA	You think I look like a whore?
MAGGIE	Darling, it's a joke! For goodness sake, don't be so sensitive! Ben, will you look at the lights please?
BEN	Um . . . I don't have much . . . mobility in this.

(GRACE *wanders in, eating something She is staring at her phone.*)

MAGGIE	Grace, darling, what happened to the lights?
GRACE	Um . . . Don't know. They just went off.

(BEN *tries to get under the tree. His costume makes it difficult.*)

DAVINA	Suits you, that outfit.
MAGGIE	Yes, you're a cute little penguin.
GRACE	Thanks.

(GRACE *moves to leave but* DAVINA *takes her hand, then hugs her.*)

DAVINA	(*grinning*) So, what d'you think of the news, Mum?
MAGGIE	Yes. I know. Wonderful news, darling.
DAVINA	You're going to be a great-grandmother.

(*Pause.*)

MAGGIE	Yes. (*She manages to smile briefly.*) Careful with the presents, Ben.

(GRACE *extricates herself from* DAVINA *and exits to the house.*)

BEN	Are we sure he'll be okay tomorrow?
MAGGIE	(*beat*) Sorry? Who?
BEN	Dad. How can we be so sure?
DAVINA	What did the doctors say?
MAGGIE	(*beat*) Sorry?
DAVINA	When you saw them this morning. What did they say exactly?
MAGGIE	He'll be fine. I'm sure. (*Beat.*) I don't understand half of what they tell me. Most of them can't speak English.
DAVINA	They all speak English, Mummy. Some of them have accents.
MAGGIE	Well, they've all got their own language, haven't they? All that . . . medical jargon . . .
DAVINA	What did they say exactly?
MAGGIE	It's fine. We'll pick him up tomorrow.
	(MAGGIE *leaves, scowling slightly.* BEN *emerges from under the tree.*)
BEN	I don't think I can play the piano in this.
DAVINA	Don't then.
BEN	Mum wants me to accompany her later.
DAVINA	Really?
BEN	It's supposed to be a surprise.
DAVINA	What is she singing?

BEN   'Have Yourself a Merry Little Christmas'.

DAVINA   Oh. Dad's favourite. Maybe you can play it
         tomorrow. When he's here.

BEN   Sometimes, I think that's the only reason Mum
         wanted me to learn piano. So I could accompany her
         at parties. Actually, I'm glad Dad isn't here. He's
         better off in hospital.

DAVINA   (*disapproving*) Ben.

BEN   He doesn't really like these things, does he?

DAVINA   That's not true.

BEN   He just goes along with it to keep Mum happy. And
         then he sits in a chair watching her make a fool of
         herself.

DAVINA   I think you're projecting.

BEN   There was more than one party when I found him in
         his shed. He'd escaped.

DAVINA   Ben, it's Christmas Eve. Please can we all be nice?
         (*Beat.*) Actually, I want to talk to you for a minute.

         (DAVINA *closes the door to the house in
         conspiratorial fashion.*)

DAVINA   You know I've been seeing a therapist.

BEN   Yes. Mum mentioned. She's not best pleased.

DAVINA   I've been learning about narcissism. And it's really
         interesting.

BEN   (*over*) Why? Because of Mum?

DAVINA   (*beat*) Yes. Because of Mum. Why else?

BEN   No. Sure. I know she has . . . tendencies.

(DAVINA *stares at him.*)

DAVINA   Ben, she's dressed as the Mother of Christ. (*Beat.*)
            Anyway, it's really interesting. Apparently,
            Christmas is notoriously difficult for narcissistic
            families. I mean, obviously it's a nightmare for
            most families because everyone has to spend time
            together and there's all this pressure, you know, to
            have a great time. But, for the narcissistic family, it's
            even worse.

BEN   What d'you mean 'family'?

DAVINA   D'you remember when Grace was a little girl? There
            were two or three Christmases here when Mum got
            drunk and ruined it for everyone. I think it's because
            she wasn't the centre of attention. (BEN *digests this.*)
            Christmas is about being part of a group, isn't it?
            A member of a family. If anyone's singled out for
            attention, it's the kids. So, for the adult narcissist,
            that's really tough. Sometimes, if they can't get the
            attention by being nice, then they get it by acting
            out.

BEN   (*sceptical*) Right.

DAVINA   Makes complete sense to me.

            (DAVINA *continues tidying the room.*)

BEN   I'm not sure. I think, maybe that was more about
            being a grandmother. She was never very keen on
            that, was she?

DAVINA   No. Because she sees it as some kind of . . .
            demotion. It's like I was promoted to the role of
            mother and she had to be grandmother. (*Beat.*) I
            can't believe I mentioned great-grandmother. I knew
            she'd hate that. (*Beat.*) But she called me a whore,
            so . . .

BEN   What d'you mean by 'narcissistic family'?

(DAVINA *stops tidying and stares at* BEN. *Pause.*)

BEN What?

DAVINA I just can't believe you bought that costume. For one thing, Grace is vegetarian.

BEN I told you. This was all they had.

DAVINA Seriously?

BEN They certainly didn't have a nut loaf costume. What did you mean by 'narcissistic family'?

DAVINA Sorry?

BEN You said Christmas is difficult for 'narcissistic families'.

DAVINA Oh. Yes, well, some would say it's a bit . . . naïve to think you could get away with it, completely. If you're raised by a narcissistic parent, you're going to inherit some traits. (*Beat.*) And the first step, as usual, is about recognising that. Taking responsibility. (*Pause.* DAVINA *continues tidying.*) It's the first step in . . . potentially, a long journey. Which is about . . . you know, reclaiming yourself.

BEN Personally, I think narcissism is the least of my worries.

DAVINA (*beat*) Okay.

(BEN *stares at her.*)

BEN You think I have 'narcissistic traits'?

(MAGGIE *enters in a bad mood.*)

MAGGIE What's the matter with that girl?

DAVINA (*beat*) What d'you mean?

MAGGIE	She's so monosyllabic. Was she out late last night?
DAVINA	Um... Not very. She had a great time. Apparently. Met up with some old school friends.
MAGGIE	I expect she was drinking.
DAVINA	No. She wasn't.
MAGGIE	How do you know?
DAVINA	Because she's not stupid.
MAGGIE	(*to* BEN) Are the lights working?
BEN	No. Sorry. They're too old. They're knackered.
MAGGIE	Ben, we have to have lights! (BEN *stares, shrugs.*) Is it the fuse? Did you change the fuse?
BEN	It's nothing to do with the fuse. They're dead. Okay?

(BEN, *irritated, exits to the house.* MAGGIE *contemplates the unilluminated tree.*)

MAGGIE   For goodness sake . . .

(*The phone rings.* MAGGIE *answers it.*)

MAGGIE   Hello? (*Pause.* MAGGIE *is frowning.*) Sorry? Who is this?

(MAGGIE *exits to the kitchen.*)

MAGGIE   (*off*) Yes, speaking. Who is this?

(DAVINA *sits and tries to relax. Then begins, quietly, reciting an affirmation.*)

DAVINA There is nothing . . . I can do to change my mother. (*Beat.*) I can never be good enough. (*Beat.*) Perfect enough. She's not capable.	MAGGIE (*off*) Sorry? I'm coming tomorrow. (*Pause.*) Tomorrow. Sorry? Can you speak up? (*Pause.*) Why do you want me to come now? (*Beat.*)

She is not capable . . . (*Beat.*) Of loving me. Consistently. Unconditionally. (*Pause. She tries to eavesdrop on* MAGGIE'S *phone call for a moment, then returns to her own thoughts.*) She is not capable. (*Beat.*) But this has nothing to do . . . (*Beat.*) This has *nothing* to do . . . With my value as a human being.

Why? What's happening? (*Beat.*) I told that doctor, the young one, Evans or . . . The young one. We agreed I'd pick him up tomorrow. (*Pause.*) Yes, I know he's ill. You don't have to . . . (*Pause.*) Okay. (*Beat.*) Yes. All right. (*Beat.*) Yes. I will. (*Beat.*) Yes. Yes, I'll come now.

(*Silence for a few moments, then* MAGGIE *enters with her shoes. She sits and begins putting them on.*)

DAVINA   What are you doing?

MAGGIE   I'm going to pick him up. I won't be long.

DAVINA   What? What did they say?

MAGGIE   I've no idea what they said. *So* infuriating . . .

DAVINA   You can't go like that.

MAGGIE   Yes, I can. It's fine. I'll only be a few minutes.

DAVINA   Mummy, you've been drinking.

MAGGIE   No, I haven't. Not much. You can drive, if you like.

DAVINA   I've been drinking too.

MAGGIE   Oh, for heaven's sake.

(MAGGIE *continues to get ready.* BEN *enters.*)

DAVINA   Ben, can you take us to the hospital, please?

BEN   Sorry?

MAGGIE   (*irritated*) No, it's fine.

DAVINA   Please can you drive us to the hospital?

BEN   No. Not like this.

MAGGIE   I won't be long.

            (*She leaves the room swiftly.*)

DAVINA   Ben, I think we're just picking him up. You can wait
            in the car.

BEN   What's the big hurry?

DAVINA   Ben! Come on. Quick!

            (DAVINA *runs after* MAGGIE. BEN *sighs and follows
            them.*)

Scene Two

Much later that night. PETER, *in sober smart-casual clothes, is
sitting on the sofa, deep in thought. Noises off.* PETER *gets up and
approaches the door to the house as* MAGGIE *enters, followed by*
DAVINA. *They are both still in costumes, though may have partially
removed or disguised them.*

MAGGIE   Hello, Peter.

PETER   Mags. Hello.

            (MAGGIE *shuffles unsteadily into the kitchen.*)

DAVINA   Hi.

PETER   (*to* DAVINA) I'm so sorry. For your loss.

DAVINA   Thanks, Peter. Thanks for coming over.

PETER   Oh! Not at all. It's a two-minute walk. How is she?

DAVINA	They think she's just a bit . . . hypoglycaemic. They suggested running a few tests but she just wanted to come home. Where's Grace?
PETER	In bed.
DAVINA	(*beat*) Oh, Okay.
PETER	We talked for a while but . . . She seems very tired.
DAVINA	Yes.
PETER	We didn't know how long you'd be.

(MAGGIE *enters with a glass of water.*)

DAVINA	Would you like something to eat, Mummy?
MAGGIE	No, thank you.
DAVINA	A mince pie, or . . .

(MAGGIE *exits to the house.*)

DAVINA	I think she should eat something.
PETER	I'll go and check her over. (*He collects his medical bag.*) Where's Ben?
DAVINA	Still in the car, I think. He said he needed a minute. Peter? (*She touches his arm. He stops, notices the contact.*) In the car, she asked me if I had any sleeping pills.
PETER	Oh, right.
DAVINA	And I said 'no'. Although I do.
PETER	Do you?
DAVINA	Yes, I've still got some Zopiclone. For emergencies. But I don't really want Mum taking them.

PETER   It's not a benzodiazepine.

DAVINA   No, but it's still addictive, isn't it?

PETER   Um . . .

DAVINA   I don't want her switching from a benzo addiction to a Z-drug addiction.

PETER   No. Sure.

DAVINA   If we end up back in rehab . . . I don't think I could stand that.

PETER   No. We won't. Don't worry about that.

DAVINA   And there's always side effects with Mum. Whatever she takes, she reacts badly. (*Half smile.*) Always a drama . . .

               (BEN *enters, still in full costume, with solemn expression.* PETER *is thrown by the costume for a moment but quickly regains composure.*)

PETER   Ben. I'm so sorry. For your loss.

BEN   Thanks.

               (BEN *sits and stares into space.* PETER *is not sure what to say, whether to comment on the costume.*)

PETER   I better check on your mother.

DAVINA   Yes. Okay. Thanks, Peter.

               (PETER *exits..* DAVINA *and* BEN *sit in silence for a while.* DAVINA *throws an occasional glance at him.*)

DAVINA   Will you take that off, please? You're not naked under there, are you?

BEN   Almost. (*Pause.*) I'm a bit pissed off. To be honest.
             (*Pause.*) One of the doctors . . . The tall one. Blond
             hair.

DAVINA   Oh, yes.

BEN   He told me that he talked to Mum this morning. Told
             her Dad was in the last stages.

DAVINA   (*beat*) Really?

BEN   He said he made it as clear as he could.

DAVINA   But she doesn't take things in. That's the problem.
             She hears what she wants to hear. (*She takes one of
             her 'Christmas pills'.* BEN *watches her.*) Propranolol.
             Do you want one?

BEN   No, thanks.

             (*Pause.* DAVINA *gets up.*)

DAVINA   I better see if she needs anything. (*She walks
             towards the door but hesitates and observes* BEN.)
             Are you okay?

BEN   Yes. (*Beat.*) Thanks.

             (DAVINA *exits to the house.* BEN *begins to cry.
             Soon* GRACE *enters. She is red-eyed and begins to
             cry when she sees* BEN *crying. She hugs him, even
             though his costume gets in the way.*)

GRACE   Are you okay?

BEN   (*beat*) Yes. I'll be fine.

             (BEN *sits, composes himself. She sits next to him.*)

BEN   I just wish I hadn't been wearing this. (*Pause.*) We
             were all sitting there. (*Beat.*) Around his bed. And
             Dad was . . . out of it really. On morphine. But there
             was a moment when . . . (*Deep, laboured breath.*)

He looked up. And looked straight at me. (*Pause.*)
He was definitely looking at me. Sitting at the end of
his bed. In a turkey costume.

(GRACE *tries to repress a laugh but fails.*)

GRACE   I'm *so* sorry!

BEN   No, it's okay.

GRACE   I'm really . . . God, I'm so sorry!

BEN   No, you're right! It's funny! (*He tries to smile but
            fails.*) It's ridiculous. It really is. (GRACE *controls
            herself.*) I don't know what was going on in his
            head.

GRACE   No.

BEN   But I felt like the world's biggest idiot. (*Beat.*) And
            then he died.

            (*Pause.*)

GRACE   (*struggling for words*) Well, it's good that . . . you
            know, that you were all there . . .

BEN   Yes. (*Pause. He gets up.*) I have to get out of this
            thing.

GRACE   Ben, I'm so sorry. I don't know why I . . .

BEN   No, it's fine! Really! (*He smiles weakly.*) It's fine.
            Not a problem.

            (*He shuffles out to the house. Left alone in the room,*
            GRACE *silently berates herself as the lights fade.*)

ACT TWO

A year later. It is late at night. Christmas detritus (used plates, glasses, empty wine bottle, nuts, chocolates, etc) is strewn around the room. A framed photograph of Donald sits amongst the Christmas cards. No fancy dress this year. A subdued atmosphere. The Christmas tree fairy lights are flashing.

MAGGIE, a glass of sherry in one hand, is half-dancing to 'Silver Bells' by Dean Martin. BEN, drinking beer, is watching his mother, mildly embarrassed. DAVINA, looking a bit stressed, is walking in and out of the kitchen, clearing up plates etc.

MAGGIE   Ben, darling, please can you stop the lights flashing?

BEN   I've tried.

MAGGIE   They're brand new!

BEN   If we had some replacement bulbs . . . We could replace the red tip flasher bulbs.

MAGGIE   The old lights are in a big bin bag in the garage.

BEN   (*not keen*) Oh. Okay.

MAGGIE   Where's Peter? Has he gone home?

DAVINA   No, he's in the lounge. He's watching Indiana Jones.

      (MAGGIE *exits.* BEN *investigates the lights. He is obstructed slightly by the large number of presents under the tree.*)

BEN   I thought we had an agreement about presents this year.

DAVINA   I didn't buy many. (*He gives her a look.*) No, I didn't. They're mostly diddies anyhow.

(BEN *switches the lights off.* DAVINA *switches the music off.*)

DAVINA   (*proclamation*) Ben, I'm really serious about this. I'm not arguing with anyone this year.

BEN   Who's arguing?

DAVINA   No, I'm just saying . . . Christmas is tough, at the best of times. And, with the anniversary of Daddy's death into the bargain . . . We all have to make a real effort.

BEN   Why are you telling me?

DAVINA   I'm not. I'm telling everyone. I talked to Grace earlier. She was getting a bit irritated with Mum.

BEN   I thought she was getting irritated with you.

DAVINA   Really?

BEN   Has she gone to bed?

DAVINA   Yes. With Zoe. They're co-sleeping.

BEN   They're what?

(DAVINA *continues clearing up.*)

DAVINA   (*wearily*) She's doing 'attachment parenting'. Co-sleeping, babywearing, you know, lots of . . . physical contact. Her father got her into it. (*Beat.*) Maybe to annoy me. He's had another baby. Did you know that?

BEN   Who? Dara?

DAVINA   He's such an idiot.

BEN   How old is he?

DAVINA	Fifty! Fifty next year. And, Claudia, his girlfriend is early twenties!
BEN	Really?
DAVINA	Twenty-six, I think. Practically Grace's age. And she's a real New Age hippie type. It's all Chakras, essential oils, crystals . . . All that garbage. And Dara just goes along with it, of course. He's so fucking wet. (*Takes a deep breath.*) Sorry! Everything about that man . . . Just winds me up.

(MAGGIE *enters.* DAVINA *puts on a smile.*)

DAVINA	Mummy, shall I make the mince pies now?
MAGGIE	Now? (*Beat.*) It's much too late, darling.
DAVINA	We have to have mince pies for Christmas Day. Don't we?
BEN	(*checks his watch*) Listen, it's almost exactly a year. Since Dad . . . um . . .
MAGGIE	Davina, I don't think moving house is a good idea.
DAVINA	Mummy, please . . . (*She checks herself, moderates her tone.*) We've talked about this. A number of times.
MAGGIE	I think you'll regret it. And I don't think Grace is all that keen.
DAVINA	The offer has been accepted, so . . . It's a little bit late to discuss this.

(*Pause.*)

BEN	Should we all . . . you know, raise a glass? (*He prepares to raise his glass of beer.*)
MAGGIE	Which house? Is it the one in a graveyard?

DAVINA   It's next door to a church.

MAGGIE   And a graveyard. There's no way I could live next to
              a graveyard.

              (BEN *sips his beer, then exits to the house.*)

MAGGIE   Is it a Jehovah's Witness church?

DAVINA   No, it's C of E. Why?

MAGGIE   Your boyfriend's a Jehovah, isn't he?

DAVINA   What? Oh, you mean Geoff? No, I'm not with him
              anymore.

              (DAVINA *exits to the kitchen.* MAGGIE *sits on the
              sofa.*)

MAGGIE   I can't keep up with all your . . . dalliances.

              (*Pause. Noises from the kitchen as* DAVINA *prepares
              to make mince pies.*)

MAGGIE   Do you still believe in Christmas?

              (*Beat.*)

DAVINA   (*off*) Why wouldn't I?

MAGGIE   Jehovah's Witnesses don't, do they?

              (DAVINA *enters.*)

DAVINA   Mummy, I'm not a Jehovah's Witness. Religion isn't
              sexually transmitted.

              (MAGGIE *grimaces and begins searching for
              something in her handbag.*)

MAGGIE   I don't know why you're so keen. On men. (*Beat.*)
              I don't know why everyone's so obsessed with sex
              these days.

(DAVINA *observes* MAGGIE *taking a pill.*)

DAVINA   (*slightly concerned*) What is that?

MAGGIE   Don't worry. It's only a placebo. (*Beat.*) Peter gave them to me.

DAVINA   How d'you know they're placebos?

MAGGIE   He told me.

DAVINA   (*beat*) He told you . . . ?

(MAGGIE *looks at* DAVINA.)

MAGGIE   Did you know?

DAVINA   (*beat*) Know what?

MAGGIE   Did you discuss it with him?

DAVINA   No. How would I know? Why is he giving you placebos?

MAGGIE   Even so, I had a bad reaction to them.

(DAVINA *stifles a sigh.*)

DAVINA   Mummy, you can't have a bad reaction to placebos.

MAGGIE   Well, I did. I couldn't sleep for a week.

DAVINA   That must be a coincidence.

(DAVINA *returns to the kitchen.*)

MAGGIE   Anyway, I know from experience. There's a big sacrifice. Inevitably. If you move away from friends, family. (*Beat.*) These things become very important, as you get older.

DAVINA   (*off*) I'm not old.

MAGGIE   I said 'older'. (*Beat.*) You're no spring chicken
                anymore, darling.

                (*Pause.*)

DAVINA   (*off*) Mummy, you can visit me. I'm about . . . two
                miles from the beach.

MAGGIE   I couldn't sleep next to a graveyard.

                (DAVINA *enters again, with rolling pin and, behind
                her back, mimes bashing her on the head with it.*)

DAVINA   What happened with Oliver, anyway?

MAGGIE   Who?

DAVINA   Oliver. You had lunch.

MAGGIE   Oh, Noddy Holder. Yes, we had lunch. It was . . .
                perfectly pleasant. I suppose.

DAVINA   He doesn't look like Noddy Holder.

MAGGIE   Yes, he does. I almost asked for his autograph.

DAVINA   I don't know what you mean. Are you seeing him
                again?

                (MAGGIE *looks at her.*)

MAGGIE   Why? (*Pause.* DAVINA *shrugs.*) I'm not short of
                friends.

DAVINA   (*beat*) No. I know.

MAGGIE   (*scrutinising her*) You didn't imagine he'd be
                anything more than a friend, did you?

DAVINA   Um . . . No. (*Beat.*) I don't suppose so.

(MAGGIE *is still staring.* DAVINA *retreats to the kitchen.* MAGGIE *sits back into the sofa and shakes her head with a malevolent expression. Pause.*)

DAVINA   (*off*) I just thought you two might have a lot in common. You're both recently bereaved . . .

MAGGIE   I've got more than my fair share of friends who are recently bereaved, thank you very much.

(MAGGIE *leaves the room. In the kitchen,* DAVINA *is unaware that* MAGGIE *has gone.*)

DAVINA   (*off*) Anyway, I've been working much too hard. As you know. And the new job will be less stressful. As far as I can tell. I'll certainly have more time at home. (*Beat.*) And the sea air and all that. I really need to relax. And unwind for a bit. You know? (*Beat.*) It'll do Grace the world of good too.

(*Pause.* DAVINA *enters, wiping her hands with a tea towel. She discovers she has been talking to herself. She sits heavily with a sigh. Soon,* BEN *enters with an empty glass and walks into the kitchen.*)

DAVINA   Where's Mum?

BEN   (*off*) Watching the film.

(*Pause.*)

DAVINA   I think I made a mistake setting her up with Oliver.

BEN   (*off*) Who?

(*Pause.* BEN *enters, glass refilled with beer.*)

BEN   Oh, you mean Noddy Holder?

DAVINA   He doesn't look like Noddy Holder.

BEN   I can't see them as a couple.

DAVINA   She's not good with illness. That's the problem.

BEN   Is he ill?

DAVINA   He's got prostate cancer. But he's got all his own
           teeth. That's all she told me. He has to have his own
           teeth. She's not interested in sex or anything.

BEN   (*grimaces*) Do you mind?

           (BEN *exits to the house.*)

DAVINA   She's got very prudish, in her old age. (*Beat.*) But
           she's lonely. She needs a companion.

           (DAVINA *looks around and discovers she's talking to
           nobody again. She gets up slowly, then walks over
           to the framed photograph of her father.* PETER *enters
           with a purposeful expression. She is unaware of
           his presence as she contemplates the photo.* PETER
           watches her for a few moments.)

PETER   Is that Donald?.

DAVINA   (*turns*) Oh, hi. Yes, it is. (*Offers it to* PETER.) My
           favourite of him, I think.

           (PETER *takes the photo and studies it fondly.* DAVINA
           begins reading some of the cards.)

           'Maggie and Donald'. (*She looks at another card.*)
           'Donald and Maggie'. She said she'd inform
           everyone. But she hasn't. (*Beat.*) I suppose I'll have
           to do it. Like everything else. (*Heavy sigh.*) I can't
           wait to get away from here. (*Beat.*) From everything.
           Everyone.

PETER   Including me?

           (*He touches her hair.* DAVINA *moves away.*)

DAVINA   No. I'm just finding it difficult being with Mum.
            Increasingly. Why did you tell Mum they were
            placebos?

PETER   Um . . . (*Pause. He shrugs.*) She asked what they
            were.

DAVINA   (*repressing irritation*) What's the point of giving her
            placebos if you're going to tell her what they are?

PETER   Actually, there's evidence for efficacy even when
            patients know what they're taking. (DAVINA *is
            staring, frowning.*) Something to do with the
            performance of a medical ritual. Like you said, she
            loves taking pills.

DAVINA   It's not what we discussed.

PETER   No. Sorry. (*Shrug.*) Professionally speaking . . .
            There are ethical problems with . . . deception.

DAVINA   Well, we have to lie to each other in our family.
            Otherwise, life would be unbearable.

PETER   If it doesn't work, we can try her on a low dose of
            Mirtazapine or something.

DAVINA   (*beat*) I don't know . . .

PETER   The new drugs are a million miles away from the old
            benzos.

DAVINA   (*thinking*) Yes.

PETER   Or we can give her something homeopathic. The
            modern-day placebo.

            (MAGGIE *enters with a suspicious expression.*)

MAGGIE   What's going on in here? I hope you're not making
            mince pies, Davina.

DAVINA   Um . . . I made a start.

MAGGIE   Will you please go to bed?

              (DAVINA *stares at* MAGGIE, *then* PETER. *She raises her*
              hands, wearily, in surrender and leaves the room.)

DAVINA   Good night, Peter. Happy Christmas.

PETER   Yes. You too. Good night.

              (*Glances between* PETER *and* MAGGIE. *Then* MAGGIE
              contemplates the presents under the tree.)

MAGGIE   I dread to think what's in all these.

PETER   You 'dread to think'?

MAGGIE   Lots of expensive, exotic gifts, I imagine. She
              always goes over the top. She does all this business
              travel during the year and buys things along the way.

PETER   Oh. I see.

MAGGIE   Last year it was chocolates from Belgium, silk
              shawls from India. Earrings from . . . goodness
              knows . . . Hong Kong, I think.

PETER   Crikey.

MAGGIE   Always reminds me of Christmases when I was a
              little girl. One year, I got a stocking with an orange,
              a bar of soap . . . Some writing paper, I think. (*Beat.*)
              Nothing, really, that I couldn't have picked up from
              visiting different rooms in the house.

PETER   (*chuckles*) Times have changed.

MAGGIE   Kids are so spoilt, these days. Especially at
              Christmas. It's all about Santa, isn't it? Not Jesus.

PETER   I know what you mean.

(MAGGIE *picks up one or two presents and reads the label.*)

MAGGIE It's partly guilt, of course.

PETER (*beat*) How d'you mean?

MAGGIE She's always showered Grace with gifts to compensate for not being around that much. For the fact that Grace was raised by a succession of nannies. You know, she had a Polish accent for a while. (PETER *smiles slightly, has heard this before.*) Used to say 'mumia'. Polish for mother. 'Mumia, mumia.'

PETER I'm sure it's not easy, being a single mother.

MAGGIE Did I tell you about that time I had to pick Grace up in the middle of the night?

PETER Yes. I think so.

MAGGIE She was thirteen years old. Davina dropped her at a party and then drove to a boyfriend's house. She claimed there was no reception, but . . . Grace called me. Three in the morning! She was wandering the streets! Lost!

PETER Yes, you did tell me.

MAGGIE Did I? Well, anyway, I'll never forget that look on her face, when I found her hiding in a darkened doorway. Like a little waif and stray.

(MAGGIE *begins fiddling with an iPod which is sitting on a substantial iPod dock. Her sight is not good so she has to stare at it from only a few inches away.*)

MAGGIE Shall we have some music?

PETER (*hesitates*) Okay. Sure. Although, I better go soon.

MAGGIE   She's a constant worry to me, that girl. (*Beat.*) She
            can't keep a man for longer than a few months.
            (*Beat.*) I think they get fed up because her career
            comes first. Always has. (*Beat.*) A few weeks ago,
            she set me up with this little man who looks like
            Noddy Holder. He's got prostate cancer. Kept going
            to the toilet. In the end, I just paid the bill and left
            him in there. (*Beat.*) God alone knows what she was
            thinking. (*Beat.*) But, I'll rise above it. I don't want
            to spoil Christmas.

PETER   Is that an iPod?

MAGGIE   Yes, it's Donald's. Davina had to show me how to
            use it. *And* how to work the television! There were
            weeks and weeks after he died, I couldn't watch the
            television! Amazing how complicated . . .

            (*Christmas music is heard, at modest volume. Ella
            Fitzgerald, 'Winter Wonderland'.*)

MAGGIE   This is Donald's Christmas playlist.

PETER   Oh, really?

            (*She puts a smile on her face and tries to get* PETER
            to dance.)

MAGGIE   How's your waltz these days?

PETER   Oh . . . Rusty.

            (MAGGIE *begins to lead him in a vague waltz around
            the room.* MAGGIE *sings along to the song, half-
            remembering the words. She loses her balance
            slightly.*)

PETER   Are you okay?

MAGGIE   Fine, thanks. Pleasantly drunk.

PETER   How are the um . . . the pills? How are you getting
            on with them?

MAGGIE   Oh, fine, I think. I had one or two . . . negative side effects . . . initially.

PETER   Such as?

MAGGIE   Oh, nothing much. Um . . . Insomnia. And a bit of . . . mild suicidal ideation. (PETER *stops dancing, studies her expression.*) Nothing serious. Maybe it was nothing to do with the pills.

PETER   Possibly, a slight nocebo reaction.

MAGGIE   A what?

PETER   Nocebo. Negative effects caused by negative expectations.

(*They continue dancing.*)

MAGGIE   Well, anyway, I'm fine now. And I feel all right. Generally speaking. (*Re, the music:*) We need something a bit slower, don't we?

(MAGGIE *returns to the iPod and, with some difficulty, begins scrolling through the playlist.*)

PETER   I suppose I should be going.

MAGGIE   'Merry Little Christmas' or something like that. (*Pause. Casually:*) Also . . . (*Beat.*) I don't suppose this is anything to do with the pills. But, you know I said I've had no libido for ages . . . years . . .

PETER   Oh, yes.

MAGGIE   (*still with her back to* PETER) Well, it came back. (*Beat.*) With a vengeance.

PETER   Oh, really?

                          (*Pause. She turns to look at him. He meets her gaze.
                          Then she turns back and pretends to busy herself
                          with the iPod.* PETER *is not sure what to say.*)

PETER   (*finally*) How do you feel about that?

                          (*Pause. We hear the beginning of another Christmas
                          song, then another, as* MAGGIE *flicks through. Then
                          silence again.*)

MAGGIE   I'm not sure.

PETER   It's perfectly normal for it to . . . wax and wane.
                          (*Pause.*) But, if it bothers you . . . There are one or
                          two options. (*Pause.*) Like chasteberry. Or possibly
                          progesterone. (*Beat.*) Might just . . . take the edge
                          off.

                          (*Pause. Heavy silence. Then* MAGGIE, *frowning,
                          continues to play Christmas songs in quick
                          succession, clicking from one to the next before
                          they've really begun.*)

MAGGIE   Most of these are frightful, aren't they?

                          (*More song intros.*)

PETER   Mags?

                          (MAGGIE *ignores him. She finally allows a song
                          to play. John Lennon, 'Happy Christmas (War is
                          Over)'.*)

MAGGIE   Donald was a huge Beatles fan.

                          (*She turns it up loud.*)

PETER   Is that . . . a bit too loud for Grace? And the baby?

                          (MAGGIE *turns it down but it is still fairly loud. She
                          walks towards the kitchen without looking at* PETER.)

MAGGIE   Another drink?

PETER   Oh. No, thanks.

                (MAGGIE *exits to the kitchen.* PETER *is left alone. He
                decides to turn the music down further but doesn't
                know how to. Soon,* DAVINA *enters, dressed for bed.*)

DAVINA   (*annoyed*) Mummy!

                (MAGGIE *enters with a glass of sherry.*)

MAGGIE   Sorry. (*She switches the music off.*) I suppose I
                should go to bed.

                (MAGGIE *exits to the house, almost bumping into*
                GRACE.)

MAGGIE   (*subdued*) Goodnight, darling. Merry Christmas.

                (GRACE *is tired, stressed and annoyed. She begins
                searching the room.*)

PETER   (*to* DAVINA) Sorry about that.

DAVINA   That's okay.

                (PETER *exits to the kitchen.*)

DAVINA   What are you looking for?

GRACE   Her dummy. The yellow one.

DAVINA   She's got a dummy. It's in her mouth.

GRACE   She likes the yellow one.

DAVINA   Sweetheart, you're very tired. Why don't you put
                Zoe's cot in the spare room?

GRACE   Mum, don't start.

DAVINA   Has she finished feeding?

GRACE (*beat*) Probably not.

(*Pause.*)

DAVINA You know, most mothers don't breastfeed at all after six months.

GRACE Not listening.

(DAVINA, *frowning severely, watches* GRACE *searching the room.* PETER *enters with a glass of water and hovers uncomfortably in the background.*)

DAVINA He knew very well that we'd argue about this.

GRACE What?

DAVINA Attachment parenting. He knows it's not my thing. He knew we'd argue.

(GRACE *stops and stares at* DAVINA, *then notices* PETER.)

PETER Sorry. Excuse me.

(PETER *exits to the house.*)

GRACE Dad's got nothing to do with it.

DAVINA He gave you a book.

GRACE Yes, because I asked him! I asked if I could borrow it! You think he did it to annoy you?! Seriously?!

DAVINA I wouldn't put it past him.

GRACE That's completely mental. Listen, I'm not talking anymore. (*She continues searching.*) Nan's already had a go at me today.

DAVINA What?

GRACE So, that's it! Okay? I've had enough!

DAVINA	What did she say?
GRACE	Told me I shouldn't sleep with Zoe.
DAVINA	Oh, well, it's none of her business. I'll tell her to keep her nose out.
GRACE	No! Don't! Just keep your own nose out! (*Stops searching.*) God knows where it is . . . Fucking thing.

(*She leaves the room in a hurry. Soon,* PETER *enters in overcoat and shoes.*)

PETER	I'll be off, then, Davina.
DAVINA	Her father walked out on us when she was six months. What the hell does he know about 'attachment parenting'? (*Beat.*) I expect it's Claudia's idea. And he just goes along with it. He's such a . . . spineless creature.
PETER	(*Beat.*) That's your type, isn't it?

(*Looks at him.*)

DAVINA	Why are you having a go at me?
PETER	Sorry. No. I'm not. I just remember you told me you were attracted to . . . dependent types.
DAVINA	(*sigh*) Yeah, I'm one of life's caretakers. That's how Mum trained me.
PETER	I'm too independent for you. I expect.

(*Pause. They stare at each other.* DAVINA *looks out of the door to the house, checking the coast is clear.*)

DAVINA	(*lowering her voice*) It's nothing to do with that. (*Beat.*) I don't have a type anymore. If a man seems at all . . . needy. It's a big turn-off.

PETER   What then? My age?

DAVINA   No. No, not all. I just . . . I really need some space.
               (*Beat.*) I need to be on my own, for a while. Clear
               my head. (*Pause.*) Do you understand?

               (*Pause. More eye contact.* PETER, *clearly taken with*
               DAVINA, *takes her hand for a few moments, then*
               releases it. He smiles at her warmly.)

PETER   Good night. Have a great Christmas.

DAVINA   (*smile*) I'll try.

               (*He leaves.* DAVINA *thinks for a moment, then begins*
               rearranging the cushions on the sofa. She finds the
               yellow dummy under one of them. She contemplates
               it for a moment, then puts it in her pocket. She picks
               up a couple of used glasses and switches off a light.
               The room falls into semi-darkness. DAVINA *takes*
               the glasses into the kitchen. She screams offstage
               and drops a glass which smashes on the floor. She
               reverses back into the room.)

DAVINA   Mummy! For Christ's sake!

               (MAGGIE *enters, in dressing-gown, with a glass of*
               water.)

MAGGIE   Sorry.

DAVINA   What were you doing in there?

MAGGIE   I live here.

DAVINA   Were you eavesdropping again?

MAGGIE   I was just getting some water.

               (DAVINA *stares at her, wondering what she has*
               heard. Then she turns on a light and assesses the

broken glass on the floor. She tiptoes into the kitchen and begins clearing it up. MAGGIE *watches.*)

DAVINA   (*off*) For goodness sake . . . ! Gave me the fright of my life.

MAGGIE   So did you. Shrieking like a banshee.

DAVINA   (*off*) We've probably woken Zoe again.

MAGGIE   You've got to tell that girl not to sleep with her baby. It's dangerous, for one thing.

DAVINA   (*off*) Mummy, it's not really any of your business.

MAGGIE   It's 'attachment parenting', apparently. Did you know that?

DAVINA   (*off*) Yes. Of course.

MAGGIE   It sounds exactly like all that Dr Spock nonsense from the Fifties.

          (DAVINA *enters with dustpan and brush.*)

DAVINA   Mummy, I can't talk now. Please will you go to bed?

MAGGIE   You think it's gone and forgotten but it just comes back, with a different label. There seems to be an endless recycling of . . . gobbledygook.

DAVINA   It's not gobbledygook. It's a very established method of parenting. Nothing to do with Dr Spock. It's . . . John Bowlby, I think.

MAGGIE   Her idiot father gave her a book, apparently.

DAVINA   He is not an idiot, Mummy. Why do you have to be so nasty? Please go to bed.

MAGGIE   Why don't you go to bed?

DAVINA   I want to make a start on the pies.

MAGGIE   Oh, don't be ridiculous.

DAVINA   I know I won't sleep. I just want to do something
              relaxing for half-an-hour.

MAGGIE   Nobody ever eats your pies.

              (MAGGIE *moves to the door. A thought occurs to*
              DAVINA.)

DAVINA   How did you get into the kitchen anyway? I watched
              you go to bed five minutes ago.

MAGGIE   Yes, I did. And then I came down again. It's my
              house.

              (BEN *enters with his glass of beer and a string of old,
              dusty Christmas tree lights. Awkward pause.*)

BEN   You know, it's exactly a year. D'you think we should
              raise a glass . . . ?

MAGGIE   I'm going to bed. Good night, Ben.

              (MAGGIE *exits to the house.* DAVINA *is thinking hard,
              furrowed brow.* BEN *puts his glass down and begins
              trying to locate the red-tipped flashing bulb(s) on the
              tree.*)

DAVINA   I think I made a big mistake. (*Beat.*) I think she
              overheard me.

BEN   (*beat*) Saying what?

              (*Pause.* DAVINA *wanders over to a mirror on the wall
              which is almost completely obscured by Christmas
              decorations. She uncovers the mirror and stares at
              herself.*)

DAVINA   Have you noticed there are fewer mirrors in this
              house?

(*Pause.*)

BEN   She used to say this house is like a hall of mirrors.

DAVINA   Yes.

BEN   Like at the fair.

DAVINA   Except, every mirror makes her look fat. (*Beat.*) It
             gets worse, you know. As time goes on . . .

BEN   Sorry?

DAVINA   Aging is the ultimate narcissistic injury. (*Pause.*)
             When your best friend, the mirror, starts to betray
             you . . . (*Pause.*) I suppose it's inevitable, isn't it? As
             you get older. (*Beat.*) All those . . . ghastly traits . . .
             begin to dominate.

BEN   Davina, for Christ's sake . . .

DAVINA   What?

BEN   You're not even that old.

             (*She stares at him.*)

DAVINA   I'm talking about Mum!

BEN   (*beat*) Oh.

DAVINA   (*smile*) You think I have ghastly traits?

BEN   No. I don't.

DAVINA   Why would you imagine I'm talking about myself?

BEN   Because you were looking at yourself in the mirror.

DAVINA   It's not my mirror! It's Mum's mirror!

BEN   Yeah, but it's your face, isn't it? You don't see
             Mum's face in there! Do you?

DAVINA	I'm imagining what it's like for Mum looking into this mirror.
BEN	How am I supposed to know what you're imagining?
DAVINA	Do you think I look old?
BEN	No! I don't!
DAVINA	Do you think I'm narcissistic?
BEN	Oh, for fuck's sake! Sorry I spoke!

(*He yanks at the Christmas tree lights. The tree wobbles.*)

DAVINA	Careful! (*Pause.*) Sorry. I just thought it was funny.
BEN	We're all narcissistic, aren't we? (*Beat.*) The whole family. That's what you said.
DAVINA	When?
BEN	Last Christmas.
DAVINA	I don't think I said that.
BEN	You said, 'it's impossible to be raised by a narcissistic parent without acquiring some traits'.

(*Pause.* DAVINA *quickly peers into the kitchen to make sure* MAGGIE *isn't in there.*)

DAVINA	Yes. Well, that's what my therapist told me.
BEN	Do you believe everything your therapist tells you?
DAVINA	She happens to be a leading authority on narcissism.
BEN	Really? Did she tell you that herself?
DAVINA	What's your problem?

BEN   It's just a bit rich coming from you. That's all.

DAVINA   (*beat*) What does that mean?

BEN   What does your therapist say about your sports car
               and your posh clothes and your designer handbags?

               (*Pause.*)

DAVINA   Nothing. Why would she say anything? (*Beat.*) Her
               clothes are fairly posh, come to think of it.

BEN   Right. Exactly. It's everywhere. It's the age of the
               narcissist.

DAVINA   Oh. I see. (*Beat.*) Everyone's a narcissist. Apart from
               you.

               (*She exits to the kitchen.* BEN *is replacing one or two
               bulbs on the tree with bulbs from the old lights.*)

BEN   I expect she doesn't get it because she's a
               psychologist. (*Beat.*) That's one of the problems
               with psychology. You take the individual out of
               society, as if society doesn't exist. As if we're not
               social creatures.

DAVINA   (*off*) What have you been reading?

BEN   As if we don't internalise the never-ending, neo-
               liberal bullshit. Telling us that we're not citizens
               anymore, we're just consumers! And that we
               have to let the banks and the corporations run the
               world. And governments have to get out of the way.
               Because it's all about the fucking economy! Keep
               the economy growing, perpetually, that's all that
               matters!

               (DAVINA *enters, flour on her hands, and stares at
               him, transfixed.*)

BEN   So, the only remaining reason for our existence is to
               buy stuff! To make money and spend it on ourselves!
               Especially at Christmas! You know how much is
               spent on Christmas advertising? Six billion! And
               that's just the UK. You're worth it! You deserve it!
               Think only of your own gratification! Capitalism
               feeds narcissism! It *needs* narcissism!

DAVINA   Oh, my God . . .

               (*She stares at him, scrutinising. He stares back.*)

BEN   What?

DAVINA   You've been reading books. Haven't you?

BEN   (*beat*) Yes, I read books. Is that a crime?

DAVINA   Have you been preparing that little lecture?

BEN   What?

DAVINA   Have you spent the whole year thinking about this,
               reading, researching . . . just so you can win an
               argument with me?

BEN   You really think I'd spend a year thinking about
               you? That's incredibly narcissistic.

DAVINA   There are two basic types of narcissism. Grandiose
               and vulnerable. You're a classic vulnerable, covert
               narcissist. Smugly superior, and bitter that the world
               doesn't appreciate you.

BEN   Oh, that's bullshit! I'm bitter that the world is being
               destroyed by . . . rampant materialism! By people
               like you!

               (BEN *switches on the lights. They are still flashing.
               This clearly increases his annoyance.*)

DAVINA   At some point you're going to need to let it go.

BEN   Let what go?

DAVINA	The fact that I've got more money than you.
BEN	Oh, for fuck's sake! It's nothing to do with that!

(He apparently attempts to pull all the lights off the tree and the tree falls onto him.)

DAVINA	Ben!

(DAVINA helps BEN extricate himself from under the tree.)

BEN	It's okay. I'm all right.

(Pause. BEN sits and contemplates the tree. He is holding back tears. DAVINA turns off the flashing lights.)

BEN	I have to go. I can't be here.
DAVINA	What? (Beat.) What d'you mean?

(BEN cries briefly, then screws up his face and chokes back the tears. DAVINA is taken aback. She sits next to him.)

BEN	I can't be here.
DAVINA	What's the matter? (Pause.) Ben, I'm sorry. You're not a narcissist.

(Pause. He smiles briefly.)

BEN	So typical that your therapist is a leading authority. (Beat.) The best that money can buy.
DAVINA	No, not really. She's not that expensive.
BEN	Mine is utterly incompetent. (Beat.)

BEN   I told her the turkey story. (*Beat.*) I didn't want
             to, but . . . I can't get it out of my head. (*Beat.*)
             Particularly today. In this house.

DAVINA   Why?

             (*Pause.*)

BEN   Because I've felt like a failure all my life.

DAVINA   (*beat*) Oh, come on.

BEN   I don't know what makes you think I'm 'smugly
             superior'.

DAVINA   You're not a failure, Ben. That's ridiculous.

BEN   (*shrug*) On some level, I've always felt like a huge
             disappointment.

DAVINA   Seriously?

BEN   At least, since failing my grade-eight piano.

DAVINA   A 'huge disappointment'? To whom?

             (*Pause.*)

BEN   That look Dad gave me . . . (*Beat.*) When I was
             sitting at his deathbed . . . Dressed as a turkey.
             Feeling like a turkey. (*Beat.*) Like a failure. (*Beat.*)
             That withering look . . . I know I'll never forget that.

DAVINA   Ben, you've no idea what he was thinking. I doubt
             he was thinking anything very much.

BEN   I told my therapist the whole story. And she couldn't
             stop giggling.

DAVINA   (*beat*) Really?

BEN   We tried to change the subject, but . . . She couldn't
             stop. (*Beat.*) Ruined the entire session.

DAVINA   Wow. That's . . . *so* unprofessional.

BEN   She was really apologetic but . . . I can't go back there. That's it. Don't tell Mum, okay?

DAVINA   Sure. No, of course I won't.

BEN   I need a new therapist. Do you have any recommendations?

DAVINA   Um . . . Maybe.

          (BEN *lifts the tree back to vertical, with* DAVINA'S *help.* DAVINA *begins picking up baubles, etc, from the carpet.*)

BEN   I have to go. I'm sorry.

DAVINA   Really? (BEN *just stares.*) Now?

BEN   Sorry.

DAVINA   How much have you drunk?

BEN   I'll be fine. I'll call you tomorrow.

          (*He moves to leave.* DAVINA *begins searching through the presents.*)

DAVINA   Well, at least take a present for the morning.

BEN   No, thanks.

DAVINA   There's one I think you'll really like . . .

          (*She finds the present but he has gone. She sits, forlornly, with the present on her knee. Soon* MAGGIE *enters in dressing-gown.*)

MAGGIE   Did someone just leave? Was that Ben?

(MAGGIE *notices the mess under the tree.* DAVINA *begins clearing it up, putting baubles back on the tree, etc.*)

MAGGIE   What on earth . . . ?

DAVINA   He had to leave. But he'll call tomorrow. Maybe he'll come back.

MAGGIE   Why did he leave?

DAVINA   Um . . . He wasn't feeling well.

MAGGIE   What did you say to him?

DAVINA   I didn't say anything.

MAGGIE   You certainly did. I heard you rowing. What happened to the tree?

DAVINA   Nothing. Mummy, go back to bed.

MAGGIE   Why can't you keep your mouth shut for once?

DAVINA   (*riled*) It's not my fault! I didn't make him leave!

MAGGIE   What did you say to him?

DAVINA   It's actually more your fault than mine. If you want to know the truth.

MAGGIE   What d'you mean?

DAVINA   Listen, it's Christmas Eve. Let's all go to bed.

MAGGIE   How on earth is it my fault?!

DAVINA   Mummy, it's a year since Daddy died. And, being in this house . . . on Christmas Eve . . . It brings it all back.

MAGGIE   I know. I'm sure it does.

DAVINA   Particularly, the turkey costume. And all that. It's a
           very . . . difficult memory for Ben.

MAGGIE   How is that my fault?

DAVINA   (*busy with the tree*) Forget it. Forget I said anything.

MAGGIE   I didn't make him put that daft costume on!

DAVINA   No, but you didn't tell us how sick Daddy was.

           (*Heavy pause.*)

MAGGIE   What are you talking about?

DAVINA   I'm not suggesting . . . In any way. That you
           deliberately withheld things. You were clearly in
           denial.

MAGGIE   Denial?! Of what?

DAVINA   Of how ill he was.

MAGGIE   I was not in denial about anything, thank you very
           much!

DAVINA   (*losing patience*) Well, then you were just jealous.
           As usual.

MAGGIE   Jealous?!

DAVINA   Mummy, be honest for once! You always hated
           Daddy being ill. Getting all the attention.

MAGGIE   What are you talking about?

DAVINA   You know, at some point in our lives . . . It would be
           nice if you took a little bit of responsibility.

MAGGIE   What for? For being jealous?! I've never been
           jealous!

DAVINA   (*loud*) You've always been jealous! All my life!
              Jealous of me and Daddy, or me and boyfriends, or
              me and God! Any relationship which doesn't involve
              you!

MAGGIE   That's absolute nonsense!

DAVINA   No, it isn't! You know it isn't!

MAGGIE   Is that why you seduced Peter?

              (*Pause.*)

DAVINA   I didn't seduce him.

              (DAVINA, *deflated, sits and contemplates a bauble.
              Long pause.*)

MAGGIE   How long did it last?

DAVINA   I knew you were eavesdropping.

MAGGIE   I wasn't.

DAVINA   You're an expert at it. You actually went out the
              front door and walked around the house to the back
              door. Didn't you?

MAGGIE   No.

DAVINA   In your dressing gown.

MAGGIE   I just walked through here. You obviously didn't see
              me.

              (DAVINA *stares, sceptical. Then looks away. Pause.*)

DAVINA   It was very brief. (*Beat.*) Very brief. I apologise.

MAGGIE   (*beat*) What for?

              (*Pause.*)

DAVINA	I don't know. (*Beat.*) I don't know what I'm sorry for. But it was stupid. It shouldn't have happened.
MAGGIE	You don't seem to be able to help yourself.

(DAVINA *sighs.*)

DAVINA	I can't really explain it. Except to say . . .
MAGGIE	You don't have to explain it. I'm going to bed.
DAVINA	In some way . . . It felt good being close to him for a while. (*Beat.*) I've always associated him with Daddy.
MAGGIE	Why?
DAVINA	Because he was Daddy's friend.
MAGGIE	No, he was more my friend.
DAVINA	(*makes a face*) Not really.
MAGGIE	Yes, he was. We were very close.
DAVINA	For six months.
MAGGIE	No, no, even before that.
DAVINA	He was Daddy's friend. Primarily.
MAGGIE	As usual, you've no idea what you're talking about.
DAVINA	(*riled again*) Yes, I do. Because I was involved in it all. If you remember . . .
MAGGIE	Involved in what?
DAVINA	The whole thing! The whole saga!
MAGGIE	I'm so bored with this conversation.

(MAGGIE *moves to leave.*)

DAVINA	You made me lie to Daddy. When I was fourteen years old. So you could see Peter.

(MAGGIE *turns, outraged.*)

MAGGIE   How dare you?! (*Beat.*) How dare you say that?!

DAVINA   Mummy, don't try gaslighting me! Because it won't
                work these days. My memory's better than yours.

MAGGIE   'Gaslighting'?!

DAVINA   It's what you've always done! Dismissing my
                memories! Making me doubt my own sanity!

MAGGIE   Where do you get this nonsense?! From your blasted
                therapist, I suppose!

DAVINA   It's nothing to do with her.

MAGGIE   You need to stop all this therapy nonsense! It's not
                doing you any good at all!

DAVINA   No, actually, it's doing me a lot of good.

MAGGIE   For your information, your father did a lot worse!
                Than anything I did.

DAVINA   I know. You told me. You told me everything.

MAGGIE   I did not.

DAVINA   Mummy, I was your confidante! Don't you
                remember?

MAGGIE   I didn't tell you about your father having an affair
                when I was pregnant with Ben.

DAVINA   Yes, you did!

MAGGIE   He wasn't so perfect.

DAVINA   I never said he was!

MAGGIE   You slept with Peter to spite me, didn't you?

DAVINA   No! Not at all!

MAGGIE   Yes, you did! And that's why you set me up with that
            incontinent little man.

DAVINA   Who? Noddy? I mean, Oliver? Oliver's not
            incontinent; he's just got a bit of prostate cancer at
            the moment.

MAGGIE   Is that what I deserve? A funny little man? Who's
            dying?

DAVINA   He's not dying! Lots of older men have prostate
            cancer, but they don't necessarily die from it.

MAGGIE   No, because they're so old, they die of something
            else!

            (DAVINA *takes a breath, tries to control her
            emotions.*)

DAVINA   Mummy, if you remember . . . You told me you
            were through with relationships and just wanted a
            companion.

MAGGIE   Well, I don't tell you everything.

DAVINA   All you said was he has to have his own teeth.
            You've got this weird thing about false teeth, just
            because Daddy had false teeth.

MAGGIE   Have you ever slept with a man with false teeth?

            (*Pause.* DAVINA *is thrown for a moment.*)

DAVINA   I don't know. Maybe I have. Most people didn't
            know Daddy had false teeth!

MAGGIE   I knew! They fell out once when he was on top of
            me.

            (DAVINA *is shocked and appalled.*)

DAVINA   Oh, my God! Oh, my God! (*She gets up.*) What is
              wrong with you?!

              (*She exits to the kitchen with hands over her ears.*)

MAGGIE   See! I don't tell you everything, do I?

DAVINA   (*off, loud*) No. Thanks for saving that until the
              anniversary of his death!

MAGGIE   Why don't you go to bed?

DAVINA   (*off*) Have you got any other memories you could
              share with us over lunch tomorrow?!

MAGGIE   I'm sure there are corpses in your graveyard with
              their own teeth.

DAVINA   (*off*) It's not my graveyard!

MAGGIE   I'm surprised you didn't dig one up and bring it over
              for me.

DAVINA   (*off*) Just shut up, will you! For God's sake, shut up!

MAGGIE   Go to bed.

DAVINA   (*off*) No, you go to bed!

              (*Pause.*)

MAGGIE   What are you doing in there? (*Pause.*) I hope you're
              not making mince fucking pies.

DAVINA   (*off*) Zoe will never get to sleep at this rate.

MAGGIE   You shouldn't have let her have that baby in the first
              place.

              (DAVINA *enters with mixing bowl.*)

DAVINA   Do you imagine that I have control over her womb?!

MAGGIE   She's got no husband! No career! She's got nothing!
          You can't have a baby just because you want one,
          like it's a present from Santa! It's the worst kind of
          selfishness!

DAVINA   Oh, that's interesting. It's often the most selfish
          people who are most intolerant of selfishness.

MAGGIE   You think I'm selfish?!

          (DAVINA *hesitates, then returns to the kitchen.*
          MAGGIE *rises.*)

MAGGIE   I gave my life to my family! You just thought about
          your own career and your latest boyfriend!

DAVINA   (*off*) You gave your life to us, did you? Or was it the
          other way around?

          (MAGGIE *marches into the kitchen.*)

MAGGIE   (*off*) What does that mean?

DAVINA   (*off*) Mummy, I refuse to argue with you. It's
          Christmas Eve.

MAGGIE   (*off*) Stop it, will you?! Just stop it! Nobody wants
          your stupid pies!

DAVINA   (*off*) Get off! Let go!

          (*A scuffle develops offstage.*)

MAGGIE   (*off*) Leave it!

DAVINA   (*off*) Mummy, stop!

          (*Silence. A few moments later,* MAGGIE *enters with
          quite a bit of flour on her clothes. Pause.* DAVINA
          *enters, open-mouthed in indignation. She is largely
          covered in flour, including her head. Long silence.*
          DAVINA *finally sits. They glance at each other.*)

MAGGIE   If you think it's too soon, you should've said so.

DAVINA   What? What d'you mean? (*Pause.*) No, I don't. I
              don't think it's too soon.

MAGGIE   And if you think I'm too old, you should've said that
              too.

DAVINA   No, I don't, I don't, how many times? It's just . . .
              Why is it anything to do with me?

MAGGIE   I don't know.

DAVINA   Why is it my job to organise your life?

MAGGIE   I didn't ask you to. I don't want you to.

DAVINA   You made some very big hints.

MAGGIE   No, I didn't.

              (*Pause.*)

DAVINA   I need some space. (*Pause.*) It will do both of us
              good. Don't you think? (*Pause.*) I'll leave on Boxing
              Day.

MAGGIE   You can leave now. (*Pause.*) Actually, I wish
              everyone would bugger off.

DAVINA   Good night.

              (DAVINA *leaves.* MAGGIE *shuts the door to the house
              and moves a large armchair in front of it. She turns
              the Christmas tree fairy lights on. They flash. She
              turns off other lights so the room is only illuminated
              by little flashing bulbs. She turns the music back on
              and, sipping sherry, listens to 'Happy Christmas
              (War is Over)' at considerable volume.*)

              INTERVAL.

ACT THREE

Scene One

A year later. Mid-day. The room looks similar but very tidy. The photo of Donald is obscured by Christmas cards. The fairy lights on the Christmas tree are working, and not flashing. DAVINA *enters from the house with a few bags.*

DAVINA   Ben?

            (BEN *enters from the kitchen. He is wearing an apron.*)

BEN   Oh, hi! Hi. How are you?

DAVINA   Great to see you.

            (DAVINA *puts her bags down and hugs him.* BEN *is slightly thrown by the warmth and duration of the hug.*)

BEN   Where's Grace?

DAVINA   Just taking Zoe upstairs. She's sleeping, finally.

BEN   She didn't sleep in the car?

DAVINA   No. Cried through most of the journey. (*Keeps smiling.*) The house looks lovely. Oh! The lights are working!

BEN   Yes. So far, so good.

DAVINA   How fabulous! (*She holds up one of her bags.*) I've brought mince pies.

BEN   Oh, great.

            (*She takes them into the kitchen.*)

DAVINA   (*off*) Not sure why. No one ever eats them.

BEN   Oh, I will. Definitely.

DAVINA   (*off*) Do you want one now?

BEN   Um . . . No, not just yet. How have you been?

(DAVINA *returns, beaming.*)

DAVINA   Oh, great. Really great! Thanks. It's so fabulous being by the sea. I can't tell you.

(DAVINA *picks up a couple of her bags and begins unloading presents under the tree.*)

DAVINA   I've been doing a lot of yoga . . . meditation . . .

BEN   Oh, really?

DAVINA   Learning about Buddhism. Which is fascinating!

BEN   You're a Buddhist now?

DAVINA   No, I wouldn't say that. Not yet. I'm very happy, at the moment, just keeping my mind open, you know? To new experiences, new ways of . . . being, living.

(*Pause.* DAVINA'S *positivity is making* BEN *slightly uncomfortable.*)

BEN   Well, you seem like you're . . . in a good place.

DAVINA   Oh, I am! Absolutely. But it's funny. I was getting that old feeling on the journey.

BEN   What feeling?

DAVINA   Just that low-level . . . panic. You know? I'll tell you something! I'm determined not to do that thing we do. When we come home. You know, when everyone adopts roles that they've always played in the family.

BEN   Yes. Right.

DAVINA   Doesn't matter what changes you've made, what
            kind of person . . . what kind of adult you've become
            . . . You just revert back to playing that role, you
            know? Assuming that identity. The one people
            always expect.

BEN   That's very true, yes.

DAVINA   Well, I'm determined. Absolutely. I'm not doing
            that.

            (GRACE *enters, looking rather tired.*)

GRACE   Hi Ben.

BEN   Oh, hi! (*They hug briefly.*) Merry Christmas.

GRACE   You too.

            (GRACE *begins setting up her baby monitor on the
            coffee table.* DAVINA *watches her and loses her smile
            for a moment.*)

BEN   How's Zoe?

GRACE   Oh, fine. Thanks. I'm just grateful she's asleep. How
            are you?

DAVINA   Yes, how are you?! How're things?

BEN   Oh, fine. Yes. I'm fine. Thanks. (*Pause.*) Not much
            work around but . . . No, I'm fine. (*He manages a
            half-smile.*)

DAVINA   Where's Mum?

BEN   In the bath, I believe. She'll be down soon.

            (GRACE *exits to the kitchen.*)

DAVINA   How is she?

BEN   Oh, fine. Yes. (*Beat.*) All good. She's been doing
            some volunteer work . . . Did you know about that?

DAVINA   (*beat*) No. What kind . . . ?

BEN   This charity which arranges visits for lonely old
            people.

DAVINA   Oh, really? That's great. Have you been . . . spending
            some time here?

BEN   Yes, quite a bit. On and off.

DAVINA   And she's been okay?

BEN   Yes! Absolutely. (*Beat.*) Up and down a bit. As ever.
            But, no, she's been looking forward to Christmas.
            And seeing you all.

DAVINA   (*sceptical*) Really? (*Smile.*) If you say so.

BEN   No, honestly. She has. She doesn't hold a grudge or
            anything.

DAVINA   (*beat*) About what?

BEN   Sorry?

DAVINA   (*still smiling*) Why would she hold a grudge?

BEN   No, I said, "she doesn't hold a grudge".

DAVINA   We had a row but, that wasn't really my fault.

BEN   No, it's all good. As far as she's concerned. It's all . . .
            you know, water under the bridge or whatever.

            (GRACE *enters, eating a chocolate.*)

DAVINA   What would she hold a grudge about?

BEN   She doesn't. She doesn't hold a grudge.

DAVINA   (*still smiling, just*) But why would she even use that word?

GRACE   Mum, you said you wouldn't argue.

DAVINA   I'm not arguing.

GRACE   I mean with Nan.

DAVINA   Don't call her that to her face.

GRACE   I'm not stupid.

BEN   There's nothing to argue about! Honestly.

(*Pause.*)

DAVINA   Well, I don't hold a grudge either, so . . . Let's have a great Christmas for a change, shall we?

(DAVINA *has finished unloading presents and is now arranging them under the tree.*)

DAVINA   Fewer presents this year, Ben.

BEN   Oh, right.

DAVINA   You should be proud of me. I'm striving for non-attachment. Particularly to material things.

(GRACE *shakes her head slightly and exits to the house.*)

BEN   (*observing* DAVINA*'s reaction*) Peter's coming later. By the way.

DAVINA   Oh, really? (*Beat.*) Great.

BEN   Just for a drink.

DAVINA   Okay. (*Beat.*) Good.

(*Pause.*)

BEN	I must remember to ask him about those pills.
DAVINA	What pills?
BEN	Mum started taking these . . . weird yellow pills. A couple of weeks ago. Which I've never seen before.
DAVINA	Where are they?
BEN	I've got them. I'll show them to Peter.
DAVINA	Where are they? Show me.

(BEN *hesitates, then checks the coast is clear before fetching a bottle of large yellow capsules.*)

BEN	She claims they're some sort of . . . herbal thing. But she wouldn't elaborate. (BEN *hands them to* DAVINA *who inspects them.*) I asked her where she got them and she said Phil.
DAVINA	Phil?
BEN	Yeah, he's not a doctor or anything. He's just this weird bloke she meets down the King's Head.
DAVINA	Oh, Phil! Yes. He's a nurse at the hospital. The rehab unit. That's where Mummy met him.
BEN	Oh. Right. Eileen, next door, says he's a drug dealer.
DAVINA	Eileen's a nosey old cow. (*She hands the pills back.*) I expect they're homeopathy or something.
BEN	I'll show them to Peter.
DAVINA	Did she actually say that? "I don't hold a grudge"? Did she use those words?

(MAGGIE *enters, looking glamorous, followed by* GRACE *who tries to remain on the periphery.*)

MAGGIE   Merry Christmas!

DAVINA   Oh, hi, Mummy! Yes, merry Christmas!

             (DAVINA *hugs her mother. She reciprocates half-heartedly.*)

MAGGIE   How are you?

DAVINA   Oh, excellent. Thank you. And very glad to be here!

             (MAGGIE *stares at* DAVINA *as if she's an imposter.*)

DAVINA   You look well! (*Beat.*) I hear you're doing some voluntary work.

MAGGIE   Yes. I am.

DAVINA   That's fantastic!

MAGGIE   (*shrug*) Well, if Christmas is about anything, it's about other people, isn't it? Not thinking about yourself all the time.

DAVINA   (*beat*) Absolutely! I couldn't agree more.

MAGGIE   What are you taking at the moment?

DAVINA   Nothing.

MAGGIE   Is that wise?

DAVINA   Yes, it's very wise! I feel great! Never felt better!

BEN   She's a Buddhist now.

MAGGIE   What?

DAVINA   No, I'm not. I'm not a Buddhist.

MAGGIE   A Buddhist?!

DAVINA   No, I'm just . . . studying it, for my own . . .

MAGGIE   They don't like Christmas either, do they?

DAVINA   (*beat*) I wouldn't say they don't *like* it . . .

              (*Doorbell.* GRACE *exits to answer the door.*)

DAVINA   Oh, is that Peter?

BEN   (*checks his watch*) Probably.

              (MAGGIE *exits furtively to the kitchen.*)

DAVINA   (*to* BEN) Why did you mention that?

BEN   What?

DAVINA   Buddhism.

BEN   Um . . . (*Shrug.*) I don't know. Why?

DAVINA   You know what she's like.

BEN   Sorry. Was it a secret?

DAVINA   I'm not even a Buddhist. I didn't say I was a
              Buddhist.

              (GRACE *returns, grinning.*)

GRACE   Wait 'til you see this.

              (PETER *enters wearing a ludicrous 'Father Christmas
              sitting on a reindeer' costume.* DAVINA *and* BEN *are
              both very surprised and amused by it.*)

BEN   Oh, wow!

DAVINA   Oh, my God! How fantastic!

PETER   Merry Christmas!

(PETER *hugs* BEN *and kisses* DAVINA *on the cheeks.*)

DAVINA   I absolutely love it!

BEN   It suits you!

PETER   D'you think?

DAVINA   Mum? (*Peers into the kitchen.*) Come and see this.
           Where did she go?

PETER   Am I early? What time are you . . . expecting . . . ?

           (*Pause. They stare at him blankly.*)

DAVINA   Expecting who?

BEN   I don't think we're expecting anyone.

           (PETER'S *smile fades. Pause.*)

PETER   Have I got the wrong night? (*Beat.*) I was expecting
           a party. (*Beat.*) Fancy dress.

BEN   Not to my knowledge.

           (*Pause.*)

PETER   Oh. Okay. (*Beat.*) I take it I'm the butt of a joke.

DAVINA   Really?

PETER   Last week. Maggie told me you were having another
           Christmas Eve party.

BEN   Did she?

DAVINA   Did she say fancy dress?

PETER   Yes, she did. 'The sillier the better.'

           (*Awkward pause.* BEN *is trying not to smile too
           broadly.*)

BEN   Well, you've certainly . . . fulfilled the brief.

DAVINA   I think you look great, Peter! I really do.

GRACE   Hilarious.

PETER   (*managing to smile*) Well, I'm very happy to give
                you all a cheap laugh on Christmas Eve, but, if it's
                just me . . . I don't think I'll hang about.

DAVINA   Oh, Peter. Don't leave.

PETER   I'll just go and have a word with Maggie.

DAVINA   I'm not sure where she went.

                (*They both look into the kitchen.* GRACE *exits to the
                kitchen.*)

PETER   Made herself scarce, did she?

GRACE   (*off*) She's not in here.

                (PETER *walks towards the door to the house but* BEN
                remembers the pills.)

BEN   Oh! Peter? Sorry. Can I just . . . show you these . . . ?
                (*He hands the big, yellow pills to* PETER.) We don't
                know what they are. Thought you might be able to
                . . . enlighten us.

PETER   They're placebos.

BEN   Oh. Really?

DAVINA   Okay, so, Phil's not a drug dealer; he's a placebo
                dealer.

PETER   Big, yellow ones. Pretty powerful.
                Psychosomatically speaking. (*Beat.*) See you in a
                minute.

DAVINA   Okay.

              (PETER *exits to the house. Pause.*)

DAVINA   You have to be careful, Ben, not to get drawn into
              her attention-seeking spider's web.

BEN   No. Sure.

DAVINA   I've been there, done that. And very glad to have
              extricated myself. (*Beat.*) I can't tell you how great
              it feels! Such a weight off my shoulders!

              (*Noises from the baby monitor.* GRACE *enters from
              the kitchen, eating another chocolate, and strides
              towards the door.*)

DAVINA   No, darling, it was nothing. She's asleep.

              (*They listen. Some faint gurgling noises.*)

GRACE   She's awake. She's just woken up in a strange place.

DAVINA   (*assertive*) I'll go! You sit down. Relax. Talk to
              Uncle Ben.

              (GRACE *wonders whether to argue but* DAVINA *has
              gone. She collapses onto the sofa and closes her
              eyes. Awkward pause.*)

BEN   You okay?

              (*Pause.*)

GRACE   Just tired.

BEN   Sure.

GRACE   Exhausted.

BEN   Right.

              (*Pause.*)

GRACE   It's so . . . full-on. (*Beat.*) Nothing really prepares
           you.

BEN   No. (*Pause.*) There's that African saying, 'It takes a
           village to raise a child.' (*Beat.*) We seem to think one
           person can do it. Or two at the most.

GRACE   Yes. True.

           (*Pause.*)

BEN   But you've got your Mum, at least. To help out.
           (GRACE *shakes her head slightly.*) What?

GRACE   She's doing my head in.

BEN   Really?

           (*Pause. They listen to the monitor. Nothing very
           audible.*)

BEN   (*fishing*) Is the house big enough? (*Beat.*) Sometimes
           you need space. To get away from each other.

GRACE   No, it's not that. (*Beat.*) To be honest, I'd rather
           share the house with an African village.

           (BEN *chuckles, then waits for her to say more.
           Eventually she does.*)

GRACE   There are people who think before they speak. And
           there are other people who speak first and then
           wonder if it was the right thing to say. (*Beat.*) If,
           maybe, they should have kept their gob shut. For
           a change. (*Beat.*) They're tough to live with, those
           people.

           (GRACE *closes her eyes.* BEN *watches her. It looks
           like she is falling asleep.* DAVINA *enters with another
           bag of presents which she begins placing under the
           tree.*)

DAVINA   She's fine. She's very sleepy.

GRACE   Sleepy?

DAVINA   Asleep. She's asleep.

            (GRACE *picks the monitor up and puts her ear
            against it.*)

DAVINA   Grace . . . (GRACE *lifts herself wearily.*) She'll be
            asleep again in a second. I promise you. (GRACE
            ignores her.) Grace? (GRACE *continues towards the
            door.*) You don't have to be constantly at her beck
            and call.

GRACE   Wind your neck in.

            (GRACE *leaves.* DAVINA *sighs heavily, then puts the
            smile back on her face.*)

DAVINA   I don't know why I bother. I can't tell her anything.
            But, I was the same with Mum, so . . . C'est la vie.

            (*Finished with the presents,* DAVINA *remains on the
            floor, adopts a casual lotus position, and closes her
            eyes.*)

DAVINA   Anyway, I'm glad that you're . . . getting on. You
            and Mum.

BEN   Yes, we are.

DAVINA   Makes a change.

            (*Pause.*)

BEN   Actually . . . we've had some good conversations
            recently.

            (DAVINA *throws him a look, then returns to her
            meditation.*)

DAVINA   Really?

BEN   We had lunch in your favourite place last week.
            (DAVINA *frowns.*) Nice little pub. Down by the river.

DAVINA   Oh, the Swan? That's not my favourite; that's hers.
            She always flirts with the landlord in the most
            embarrassing way. She said that was my favourite?

BEN   I thought that's what she said. (*He closes the door to
            the house.*) Anyway, I didn't know about the post-
            natal depression.

            (DAVINA *looks up, then quickly checks the kitchen to
            make sure* MAGGIE *isn't eavesdropping.*)

DAVINA   It was more than post-natal.

BEN   Yes. I know. But, it sounds like everyone was
            depressed in the Sixties, Seventies. She said she had
            coffee mornings with mothers in the neighbourhood
            and they'd all be talking about Librium and Valium
            and God knows what else.

DAVINA   Yes. They were probably taking them for anxiety,
            not depression. Doctors used to hand them out like
            sweeties.

BEN   I guess nobody knew how addictive those things
            were. She said she sees little old ladies wandering
            around and wonders how many are drug addicts.

DAVINA   She told you all this over lunch?

BEN   Yes, and she confessed she was no good at being a
            housewife/mother. (DAVINA *stares.*) She was often
            lonely. Unhappy. So, she wanted her kids to be more
            than just children to her. She expected too much
            from them.

            (*Pause.* DAVINA, *feeling jealous, returns to her
            meditation.*)

DAVINA	Yes, I've heard all that before. (*Pause.*) It's a bit of a cliché, isn't it?
BEN	How d'you mean?
DAVINA	History is full narcissistic women who weren't content to be housewife/mothers and so had to live through their children.
BEN	(*beat*) What about narcissistic men?
DAVINA	Well, they're still running the world, aren't they?
	(PETER *returns. His costume gives* BEN *some more amusement.*)
BEN	Did you find her?
PETER	Yes. (*Beat.*) Thanks.
BEN	She is getting a bit forgetful. It's possible she intended to organise a party . . .
PETER	No, I get the feeling she's annoyed with me.
BEN	Really?
	(*Glances between* PETER *and* DAVINA.)
DAVINA	Ben, please can you give us a moment?
BEN	(*beat*) Oh. Sure. Okay.
	(BEN *exits to the house.*)
DAVINA	What would she be pissed off about?
PETER	(*beat*) It's obvious, isn't it? (*Pause.*) I tried to make contact a few times. The beginning of the year. But she was avoiding me. Clearly. Then I get a call, last week. She invites me to a Christmas Eve party. 'Just like old times', she said. Told me loads of people were coming. (*Beat.*) And she seemed fine. So, I

thought I was forgiven. Thought, maybe, she'd, you know, shrugged it off.

DAVINA   No. She doesn't do that.

PETER   (*re the costume*) So, I thought I better make an effort.

DAVINA   She'll be okay. She's just having a bit of a laugh, I expect. At your expense.

          (*Pause.*)

PETER   Are you all right?

DAVINA   Yes, thanks. I'm great, thanks. All good.

PETER   Are you taking anything?

DAVINA   You sound like Mum.

PETER   She said you seem a bit unbalanced.

DAVINA   (*beat*) Unbalanced? What does that mean?

PETER   (*shrug*) I've no idea.

DAVINA   Unbalanced?! You mean, like unhinged or something?

PETER   No, I don't think 'unhinged'. I think she just meant . . . you know . . .

DAVINA   Deranged?

PETER   I've no idea. You know what she's like. Sometimes she . . . projects her own mental state onto people. Listen, I need to leave. I'm really not comfortable.

DAVINA   Really?

PETER   Yes, sorry. Maybe I'll drop in on Boxing Day.
               Unless you want to come over? For a coffee. I'd
               love to . . . catch up a bit.

               (MAGGIE *enters with some carrier bags.*)

PETER   Oh. Hi. Maggie. I'm just leaving.

MAGGIE   Leaving? You've only just got here.

PETER   Well, I feel a bit stupid. To be honest.

DAVINA   Mummy, why did you tell Peter I seem unbalanced?

MAGGIE   (*beat*) Darling, give me some credit. I know you
               well enough to know when something's not right.

DAVINA   What d'you mean?! I'm absolutely fine! In fact, I've
               never been happier!

MAGGIE   All right, all right. No need to shout.

               (DAVINA *closes her eyes, takes a breath.*)

DAVINA   Honestly! I'm in a really good place.

MAGGIE   Okay. I'm glad to hear it, darling. I need to wrap
               some presents. Can I have this room for a bit?

DAVINA   Why? What's wrong with your bedroom?

MAGGIE   I don't have the floor space.

               (*Pause.* DAVINA *manages a faint smile and exits to
               the house.*)

PETER   Can I have a quick word?

               (*Pause.* MAGGIE *closes the door to the house, then
               begins to busy herself with a few presents, wrapping
               paper, scissors and Sellotape.*)

MAGGIE   I like your costume.

(*Pause.*)

PETER   Is it humiliating enough?

MAGGIE   I told you. We had a change of plans.

PETER   Mags, please can we be straight with each other?

             (*Pause.* MAGGIE *concentrates on her present wrapping.*)

MAGGIE   All right. It was a silly joke. (*Beat.*) I thought you might see the funny side.

PETER   You knew Davina would be here. You wanted to embarrass me, did you?

MAGGIE   No. Not really. (*Pause.*) I embarrassed you in front of Davina, did I? (*Beat.*) Poor Peter.

PETER   I apologise. Okay?

MAGGIE   What for?

PETER   I was in a bad place at the time. So was Davina actually.

MAGGIE   She'd have to be.

PETER   And it just happened. We just happened to be on the same . . . you know, collision course . . . (*Beat.*) It didn't amount to very much. To be honest.

MAGGIE   I'm sure she'd be pleased to hear that.

PETER   If anything, it meant less to her than it did to me.

             (*Pause.*)

MAGGIE   What about us? (*Beat.*) What did we amount to?

PETER   Mags, that's . . . forty years ago!

MAGGIE   Thirty-six.

            (*Pause.*)

PETER   Anyway, I apologise. (*Pause.*) I have to go.

            (*Pause. He moves to leave.*)

MAGGIE   D'you remember telling me you'd always love me?

            (PETER *stops. Pause.*)

PETER   I'm sure I did say that. (*Pause.*) But it's not easy to
            love someone for thirty-six years who doesn't love
            you back.

            (*Pause.*)

MAGGIE   Is that why you seduced my daughter?

PETER   Oh, come on. Seriously?! Is that what you think?!

MAGGIE   I don't know what to think. These days. About
            anything.

PETER   I didn't seduce her. It just happened.

MAGGIE   Okay. (*Pause.*) See you some time.

PETER   We both know . . . It would never have worked.
            Would it? (*Pause.*) I'm not easy to live with.

MAGGIE   No. I'm sure.

            (*Pause.*)

PETER   I don't think either of us are happy playing second
            fiddle. Are we?

            (*Pause.*)

MAGGIE   D'you think Donald was second fiddle?

(*Pause.*)

PETER   Not exactly. But he spent a lot of time in his own . . . little bubble.

MAGGIE   'Bubble'? You mean 'shed'.

PETER   (*shrug*) Well, it's a nice shed.

MAGGIE   I should have had him stuffed. So, he could sit in there for ever.

PETER   He was devoted to you.

(*Pause. He moves to leave.*)

MAGGIE   Go on, say it.

PETER   What?

MAGGIE   You're thinking 'God knows why'.

PETER   No, I'm not. I know why men fell for you.

MAGGIE   'Fell'. Past tense. (*Pause.*) Have you ever prescribed libido-lowering drugs to a man?

(PETER *is taken aback, momentarily. Pause.*)

PETER   Oh, okay. Is that another crime? For which I must be punished?

MAGGIE   No. I just want to know.

PETER   Know what?

MAGGIE   Have you ever prescribed libido-lowering drugs to a man?

PETER   Yes.

(PETER *sits and covers some of the more embarrassing elements of his costume with a cushion.*)

PETER In certain cases. (*Beat.*) Hyper-sexuality. Or . . . other circumstances . . . in which high libido is problematic.

MAGGIE Like what? Sex offenders?

PETER You gave me the distinct impression, as did Davina, that you were over it.

MAGGIE Past it.

PETER That you just wanted companionship. And that made sense to me because relationships have always made you miserable.

MAGGIE That's not true.

PETER That barrister. What's his name? When he ran back to his wife. You were in and out of hospital for a year.

MAGGIE No, that wasn't all about him. There were lots of reasons . . .

PETER Anyway, chasteberry isn't much of a drug.

MAGGIE What is it, a placebo? Another fake pill?

(MAGGIE *contemplates a yellow blouse before wrapping it.*)

MAGGIE I shouldn't have bought this. It's not her colour. Maybe I'll keep it.

PETER Mags, I'm really sorry. If I've made things . . . more difficult for you. (*Beat.*) I know how tough it is to lose someone. (*Pause.*) The first two years are the worst. In my experience. (*No response from* MAGGIE.

Pause.) I've seen you once or twice, in town, with a man . . .

MAGGIE   Graham. Yes. It didn't last. We didn't have anything in common.

(*Pause.*)

PETER   Is that essential?

MAGGIE   Yes, it is. Increasingly.

PETER   You know what, Maggie. Other people are . . . exactly that: they're other people. They're always going to be a bit 'other'. A bit separate. They can't be extensions of you.

MAGGIE   I know that. (*Beat.*) I thought you were leaving.

PETER   (*beat*) Yes. Sorry.

(*He gets up and moves to leave.*)

MAGGIE   I'm out of the game, Peter. (*Beat.*) Finally. (*Beat.*) After a lifetime of being . . . at the very least, noticed . . .

(*Pause.*)

PETER   Oh, come on.

(*Pause.* PETER *is not sure what to say.*)

PETER   (*finally*) I can drop in on Boxing Day, if that's . . .

MAGGIE   I'll call you. (*Beat.*) Merry Christmas.

(*Pause.*)

PETER   You too.

(*He leaves. Pause.* MAGGIE *won't allow herself
to cry. She forces the tears back, then continues
wrapping.*)

Scene Two

*Much later. Late at night. The room is less tidy. Amongst other
items, there is a plate of mince pies on the coffee table.* DAVINA *is
sitting on the floor, meditating.* GRACE *enters from the kitchen with
a glass of wine and a box of chocolates. She slumps onto the sofa
and sighs heavily. Pause.* DAVINA *glances at her.*

DAVINA   You should go to bed.

GRACE   I just need a couple of minutes.

            (*Pause.*)

DAVINA   Mince pie?

GRACE   No, thanks.

            (*Pause.* GRACE *becomes aware that the baby monitor
            is completely silent. She inspects it.*)

GRACE   Why is this switched off?

DAVINA   Oh! Sorry. You were up there, with her. I didn't want
            to intrude.

            (GRACE *switches it on.*)

DAVINA   It's fine. She's asleep.

GRACE   (*under her breath*) For Christ's sake . . .

            (BEN *enters and begins searching the room.*)

BEN   I've lost her pills.

DAVINA   What pills? Which pills?

BEN   Her placebos. She's searching everywhere for them.
                I must have left them in here somewhere.

DAVINA   I haven't seen them.

                (BEN *begins searching the sofa around* GRACE.
                GRACE *is clearly irritated. She gulps the rest of her
                wine.*)

GRACE   Why does everyone run around after Nan all the
                time?

BEN   (*beat*) Yes. Fair point.

DAVINA   Just be thankful that she isn't your mother.

                (*Pause.* GRACE *decides not to say anything. She
                switches off the baby monitor.*)

GRACE   (*to* BEN *as she exits*) Good night.

BEN   Night, Grace.

                (GRACE *exits. Pause.* DAVINA *starts assisting* BEN *in
                his search, though is clearly preoccupied.*)

BEN   Are you okay?

DAVINA   (*beat*) Why does everyone ask me that?

BEN   Sorry.

                (*Pause.*)

DAVINA   You know what? The older she gets, the more she
                reminds me of Mum.

BEN   Yes. I know what you mean.

                (DAVINA *looks at him. He is busy searching. Pause.*
                DAVINA *exits to the kitchen and returns with a tube
                of Smarties and an empty pill bottle. She begins*

*selecting yellow Smarties and putting them into the
bottle. Pause.* BEN *notices* DAVINA.)

BEN   What are you doing?

DAVINA   Maybe she'll take these instead. If they're all yellow.

BEN   D'you think?

           (DAVINA *shrugs and continues.*)

DAVINA   Do you want a mince pie?

BEN   No, thanks.

           (BEN *continues searching the room. Pause.*)

DAVINA   In what way does she remind you . . . ? Of Mum?

BEN   Sorry?

DAVINA   Grace. How does she remind you of Mum?

           (BEN *stops, looks at* DAVINA.)

BEN   I didn't say that. You said that.

DAVINA   Do you think she's self-involved?

           (*Pause.*)

BEN   No. I don't.

DAVINA   She gives the appearance of . . . self-confidence.
           But she's actually very down on herself. Which I
           don't understand. (*Pause.*) I don't think I could have
           done much more. (*Beat.*) She always knew she was
           loved. Unconditionally. And I was so careful not to
           . . . you know, impose expectations . . . pressures . . .
           (*Beat.*) But, it's not really what you say, is it? It's
           who you are, as a parent. What kind of role model.
           (*Beat.*) Doesn't matter how many times you say 'it's
           not your job to look after me'. The fact is, she grew

up with a mother who was anxious, self-critical, depressive, neurotic . . .

BEN   Christ, will you give yourself a break?

(DAVINA *stops what she's doing, closes her eyes, and meditates silently for a few moments. Then she continues sorting Smarties.*)

DAVINA   She's more like me, actually. She's not really like Mum at all. Unless you think I'm like Mum . . . ? Is that what you think?

BEN   I didn't say anything.

DAVINA   You said Grace reminds you of Mum.

BEN   No, you said that!

DAVINA   You agreed with me.

(BEN *raises his hands in surrender.*)

BEN   I only agreed with you because I didn't want to argue with you!

DAVINA   What?

BEN   I'm trying my best to make this a . . . relatively peaceful Christmas! For a change. So, I promised myself I wouldn't argue with anyone.

DAVINA   Oh, are you in charge now? Has Mum promoted you to . . . Director of Christmas? Senior Elf or something?

BEN   (*beat*) I don't know what you mean. I'm just trying to . . . not fall out with you.

DAVINA   How? By agreeing with everything I say?

BEN   Pretty much.

DAVINA   Even when I'm critical of my own daughter?

BEN   All you said is she reminds you of Mum. Is that a criticism?

DAVINA   Of course it is.

BEN   Okay. Well, then, I take it back.

DAVINA   She doesn't remind you of Mum?

BEN   Why are you making such a big deal of this?!

            (*Pause.* DAVINA *returns to her Smarties.*)

DAVINA   Because I've spent my life feeling not good enough. Feeling like, if something's wrong, it's probably my fault.

BEN   Well, that's bullshit.

DAVINA   No, it's not. As far as parenting goes . . . I fucked up.

BEN   No, you didn't.

DAVINA   Yes, I did. I wasn't . . . available enough. (*Beat.*) At certain times . . . I wasn't there for her.

BEN   I don't believe that.

DAVINA   In a way, it's Mum's fault. She was so . . . overwhelming . . . engulfing . . . I didn't want to do that to Grace. I was determined to let her be her own person. You know? Let her do what she wanted, within reason, go where she wanted to go. (*Pause.*) Maybe you just do the opposite of what your own parents did. Like a . . . what d'you call it, pendulum. And you just make the opposite mistakes. (*Beat.*) And now Grace is doing the opposite to me. (*Beat.*) She's all over that little girl. It's not easy to watch. (*Looks at the baby monitor.*) Or listen to. (*Pause.*) Maybe Zoe will grow up and think, 'the last thing I'm going to do to my child is . . . fucking 'babywearing''.

BEN   Not everything is about our parents, you know. We can't spend our whole lives blaming them for everything.

DAVINA   No. I know. (*Beat.*) And I don't. (*Beat.*) I blame myself too.

BEN   Right. You blame yourself for all Grace's problems and you blame Mum for all your problems.

         (DAVINA *contemplates this for a moment.*)

DAVINA   I don't blame Mum for all my problems.

BEN   Really? Since when?

DAVINA   I reckon you've spent more of your life blaming your parents than I have.

BEN   That's not true.

DAVINA   Oh, Ben! Do me a favour!

BEN   Blame them for what?

DAVINA   For not being interested in you unless you're doing something which interests them! For telling you you'd be a concert pianist if you played the piano every night after school! For making you feel like a fucking turkey!

BEN   It's not their fault that almost everything in our culture tells us that we can be whoever we want to be! (*Beat.*) And that we should think only of ourselves, and our own personal, fucking . . . aggrandisement! You only live once! Just follow your dreams! The world is your oyster! It's not just me. *Everyone* grows up . . . immersed in that bullshit! And most people don't get to be rich and

famous, don't win any medals and end up feeling
like failures for the rest of their miserable lives!

DAVINA   (*beat*) Merry Christmas.

BEN   There's this . . . *huge* fucking chasm between
           expectations and realities. (*Beat.*) And, if anything,
           it's getting worse! Young people today, can't even
           buy their own homes!

DAVINA   Yes, I'm aware of that. They have to live with their
           neurotic mothers for ever.

BEN   Oh, is that your fault too? The fact that she can't buy
           a house?

DAVINA   Will you keep your voice down please?

           (*Pause.* BEN *sits.*)

BEN   Sorry.

DAVINA   I agree with you. It is getting worse. (*Beat.*) Grace
           spends her life on Instagram, looking at pictures of
           perfect women.

BEN   Really?

DAVINA   They all do. All her friends. One of them is getting
           a boob job for Christmas. (*Beat.*) So much pressure,
           these days . . . Grace lost weight so fast after Zoe.
           (*Beat.*) I didn't do that. I was fat for years. (*Pause.*) I
           suppose I think it's my job to protect her.

BEN   How are you going to do that? Move to . . . the
           Orkneys?! Even that wouldn't work. Unless you're
           off-grid and unplugged from everything.

           (MAGGIE *enters.*)

MAGGIE   Who's moving to the Orkneys?

DAVINA   Nobody.

MAGGIE   You want to move further away?! A hundred miles
            isn't enough?!

DAVINA   Mummy, please shut up. Nobody's moving to the
            Orkneys. (*Offers her the bottle of yellow Smarties.*)
            Here. Take one of these. They're placebos. Peter left
            them.

MAGGIE   (*examines them suspiciously*) These are Smarties.
            D'you think I'm an idiot?

            (MAGGIE *leaves the room, still searching.* BEN
            continues searching agitatedly. DAVINA *eats a large
            handful of yellow Smarties and watches* BEN.)

DAVINA   She's not going to die, you know? She'll probably
            outlive us all. So, don't get sucked into worrying
            about her.

BEN   No, I'm not.

            (*He stops, sits. Pause.*)

DAVINA   I think it's done her good. Not having me around.
            It's forced her to get out into the world a bit. You
            know?

BEN   Yes. Maybe.

DAVINA   I was hoping she'd meet someone.

BEN   Oh, that's off the agenda. After Graham.

DAVINA   (*pause*) Who?

BEN   Graham. (*Beat.*) Didn't you know?

DAVINA   Who's Graham?

BEN   Retired teacher. Lives in Wolsey Road. They had a
            bit of a . . . summer fling.

DAVINA   A 'summer fling'?

BEN   He moved in for a couple of months.

              (*Pause.* DAVINA *is taken aback.*)

DAVINA   He moved in?

BEN   Yeah. He did.

DAVINA   He moved in here?

BEN   Uh-huh.

              (BEN *continues searching.* DAVINA, *thinking hard, eats a few more Smarties.*)

DAVINA   I called Mum . . . at various times, during the year. She never mentioned him. He moved in?!

BEN   Yes, but he just wanted to watch Sky Sports all day. So, she threw him out.

DAVINA   Wow. That's so typical. (*A brief smile.*) I wanted a little break and now I'm frozen out.

BEN   What d'you mean?

DAVINA   I know her too well, Ben.

BEN   I got the impression that she wanted to . . . you know, respect your need for space.

DAVINA   Oh, that's bullshit! I've heard about her private life, in appalling detail, since I was a little girl. Now she doesn't mention a live-in lover?

BEN   I assumed you knew.

DAVINA   She knew you'd mention it. And she thought I'd be jealous. But, I'm not. I'm absolutely not. I'm so over it.

(MAGGIE *enters with some of her yellow placebos.*)

MAGGIE   Don't worry, Ben, they'll turn up.

(MAGGIE *takes one.*)

BEN   Where did you get those?

MAGGIE   I've got a stockpile in my bottom drawer.

BEN   (*deflated*) Oh, right. (*Beat.*) I didn't know that.

DAVINA   What's this I hear about Graham? (*Glances between
            all three.*) Sorry, is it a secret?

MAGGIE   No, of course not. There's nothing to say.

DAVINA   He moved in. For two months.

MAGGIE   It was a mistake. That's all.

DAVINA   (*casual*) Why didn't you tell me?

(*Pause.* BEN *makes a gesture to* DAVINA, *behind
Mum's back, meaning 'drop it'.*)

MAGGIE   Why should I tell you everything?

(DAVINA *laughs briefly.*)

DAVINA   Mummy, that's hilarious.

MAGGIE   I thought you wanted a break.

DAVINA   Yes, but . . . Mummy, I called you, *regularly*. And
            told you *all* my news. Even about that affair with the
            Dyno-Rod man.

MAGGIE   I'm not sure I wanted to hear about that.

DAVINA   And I kept suggesting you call me. But you never
            did.

MAGGIE   Because I didn't think you wanted me to.

DAVINA   Just because I want a bit of time to myself . . . A bit
            of space. It doesn't mean you have to freeze me out.

MAGGIE   I haven't frozen you out!

BEN   Listen . . .

DAVINA   Okay. Never mind.

MAGGIE   I didn't ask you to call me. You don't have to call me
            at all!

DAVINA   Mummy . . .

MAGGIE   And you don't have to be here. Now that you're a
            Buddhist. There's no point celebrating Christmas, is
            there?

DAVINA   I'm not a Buddhist.

MAGGIE   I can't keep up. You were a Jehovah's Witness last
            year.

DAVINA   I was never a Jehovah's Witness!

MAGGIE   You're more promiscuous with your Gods than with
            your men.

            (DAVINA *stares. Heavy pause.*)

BEN   Folks, it's Christmas Eve. Please can we try to be
            nice?

MAGGIE   I'm just saying, she doesn't need to be here. If she
            hates Christmas so much.

DAVINA   I don't hate Christmas.

MAGGIE   You ruined last Christmas.

DAVINA   (*beat*) What?!

(DAVINA *is indignant, but grinning with incredulity.*)

BEN   Listen, let's forget about last Christmas. We all said
              things we probably regret.

DAVINA   How the hell did I ruin last Christmas?!

MAGGIE   You argued with everyone and then buggered off.

DAVINA   I didn't bugger off! Ben buggered off!

MAGGIE   You couldn't wait to leave.

BEN   I came back on Boxing Day. After you left.

DAVINA   Right! But I was here on Christmas Day! Ben
              wasn't! And we had a pretty good day, as a matter of
              fact.

MAGGIE   (*to* BEN) You were ill, weren't you?

BEN   Yes, I had some . . . stomach trouble.

DAVINA   Oh, come on! Be honest! You couldn't be here
              because of the turkey thing!

MAGGIE   What turkey thing?

DAVINA   He was dressed as a turkey at Daddy's deathbed.

MAGGIE   Yes, we all know that! He doesn't need to be
              reminded!

DAVINA   Mummy, he couldn't get it out of his head! Probably
              never will!

MAGGIE   Not with you around.

BEN   Don't blow it out of proportion.

DAVINA   Ben! For Christ's sake! You asked for my help to
              find a therapist who wouldn't laugh at you!

BEN   No, I didn't!

MAGGIE   Don't make things up!

DAVINA   Oh my God, you're both gaslighting me!

BEN   What?

DAVINA   Last year! In this room! You told me your therapist
           couldn't stop giggling! Ruined the entire session!
           And you asked if I had any recommendations!

BEN   You should be a police woman. 'Everything you
           say will be taken down in evidence and used against
           you.'

DAVINA   Well, I apologise! But it's the result of a lifetime of
           having my reality negated!

MAGGIE   Davina, that's enough!

DAVINA   Yes, it is! More than enough! I'm going to bed.

MAGGIE   Good.

           (DAVINA *gets up, prepares to leave the room.*)

DAVINA   You deserve each other! And I'm not jealous at all.
           I'm over it. I refuse to have my life defined by your
           failures.

BEN   Oh, Christ . . .

MAGGIE   What failures?

DAVINA   Oh, come on. D'you want a list?

MAGGIE   I've been a terrible mother, have I? Compared with
           you.

DAVINA   What's that supposed to mean?

MAGGIE   I never left you at night wandering the streets.

DAVINA   That was ONE OCCASION! You'll never let me forget that, will you?!

MAGGIE   And you never had a Polish accent. As far as I can remember.

DAVINA   (*loud*) Grace never had a Polish accent!

MAGGIE   "Mumia, Mumia . . . When's Mumia coming home?"

DAVINA   Oh, shut up! Just shut your mouth! You nasty old bitch!

MAGGIE   Christmas is cancelled. You can all leave.

           (MAGGIE *begins collecting up presents from under the tree.*)

DAVINA   Fine! I don't want your presents, anyway! You always buy things you'd like yourself, never anything I'd actually like!

           (MAGGIE *storms out with the presents. Brief pause, then* DAVINA *screams into her hands and hits her own head with her fists.*)

BEN   Hey! Careful.

           (DAVINA *flops into an armchair. Pause.* BEN *observes her anxiously.*)

DAVINA   It's amazing what she does to me. (*Beat.*) I was so happy before I got here. (*Pause.*) At least, I thought I was. (*Pause.*) But nobody wants me to be happy. We're all too jealous for that.

BEN   What d'you mean?

DAVINA   Even you. You're nicer to me when I'm miserable.

BEN   That's not true.

DAVINA   You don't want me to be happy. At least, happier than you.

BEN   Davina, we're all too old for all that bullshit. You know?

DAVINA   What bullshit?

BEN   Sibling rivalry, resentments, petty . . . bullshit. Believe it or not, Mum was looking forward to seeing you.

DAVINA   Will you stop taking her side? It's pissing me off. I had to listen to you slagging her off for years.

BEN   What?

DAVINA   Don't deny it!

BEN   (*beat*) No. Okay. (*Beat.*) I'm sure you've got . . . transcripts . . . memorised.

          (*Extended pause.* DAVINA *tries to meditate.*)

BEN   (*eventually*) I suppose . . . I feel like I've got to know her better. Recently.

DAVINA   Yes, I know. Your cosy little lunches. At the Swan. She knew you'd tell me all about them. (BEN *stares blankly.*) And it's fine by me. If you want to be her new confidante . . . That's fantastic. Good luck.

          (*Crash from upstairs.*)

BEN   What the fuck . . . ?

          (BEN *exits quickly to investigate. Pause.* DAVINA *turns on the baby monitor. All seems to be peaceful in* GRACE *and Zoe's room.* DAVINA *tries to relax.*)

DAVINA   There is. Nothing. (*Pause.*) I can do. To change my mother. (*Pause.*) She is not. (*Beat.*) Capable. Of . . .

(DAVINA *stops herself crying. Soon* BEN *returns, searching urgently for the phone.*)

BEN   I need to call Peter.

DAVINA   D'you mean Santa? He won't come 'til you're asleep.

BEN   She's taken an overdose.

DAVINA   (*shocked*) What?!

BEN   Her yellow pills. She's swallowed all of them.

(DAVINA'S *shock turns into bewilderment.*)

DAVINA   Her placebos? (*Beat.*) She's taken an overdose of placebos?!

BEN   Well, who knows what's in those things.

(*Zoe is heard crying over the baby monitor.* DAVINA *takes the phone from* BEN.)

DAVINA   She always manages to pull focus, doesn't she? She always upstages everyone. Well, all right, how about this? I'm taking an overdose of mince pies!

(*She begins stuffing mince pies into her mouth.*)

BEN   Davina. For Christ's sake!

(BEN *tries to retrieve the phone and the pies.*)

DAVINA   (*mouth full*) Somebody's got to eat the fucking things!

(GRACE *enters, furious.*)

GRACE   What is wrong with you?! I've had enough! I'm taking Zoe home and you can all stay here and have a miserable Christmas!

(*She stomps out.* DAVINA *gags on the pies and exits to the kitchen.* BEN *dials* PETER'S *number and waits for him to answer.*)

BEN   (*finally*) Oh, hi, Peter. Um . . . Maggie's . . . in a bit of a state . . .

           (DAVINA *storms in and snatches the phone.*)

DAVINA   No, she isn't! Peter, sorry, she's fine. We're all fine. You're better off out of it. Have a lovely Christmas.

           (*She hangs up, then collapses onto the sofa and begins sobbing.* BEN *watches, not sure what to do. He has never seen* DAVINA *cry like this. Soon,* MAGGIE *enters and exchanges glances with* BEN. MAGGIE *is also surprised, perturbed, by* DAVINA'S *uncontrolled sobbing.*)

MAGGIE   See, I knew there was something wrong.

           (MAGGIE *sits next to* DAVINA *but is not sure what to do.*)

BEN   (*to* MAGGIE) Are you okay?

MAGGIE   Yes. Thanks. I brought them all up. (*Beat.*) Davina? (DAVINA*'s sobs begin to abate.*) Darling. I'm sorry.

DAVINA   No. I'm sorry.

           (MAGGIE *begins to stroke* DAVINA'S *hair. She stops crying. Pause.*)

DAVINA   I'm sorry. I over-reacted.

MAGGIE   No, I did. As usual.

DAVINA   When I heard about . . . Graham. (*Beat.*) I don't know. It felt like I'd lost you.

MAGGIE   Lost me?

DAVINA   I've already lost Daddy. I can't lose you too.

MAGGIE   You haven't. Of course you haven't. I should have
              told you. I'm sorry.

              (GRACE *enters cautiously.*)

GRACE   What's the matter?

              (DAVINA *wipes her face, composes herself quickly.*)

DAVINA   Nothing. Sorry. I'm fine.

              (GRACE *joins her mother and grandmother on the
              sofa.* DAVINA *reaches out for her.* GRACE *takes her
              hand. Zoe begins crying again, amplified by the
              baby monitor.* GRACE *is clearly torn between Zoe and*
              DAVINA.)

MAGGIE   It's all right, darling. I'll go.

              (GRACE *is not sure but lets* MAGGIE *leave the room to
              attend to Zoe.*)

DAVINA   I'm sorry, sweetheart. I'm so sorry. You don't have
              to leave.

GRACE   I'm not leaving.

DAVINA   Oh, good. Good.

GRACE   I'm not leaving because I don't want to be alone
              with her.

              (*Pause.* BEN, *in the background, senses this is a
              mother-daughter moment and leaves the room
              silently.*)

GRACE   I don't know what to do. (*Beat.*) I'm not sure how
              much more I can take.

DAVINA   (*concerned*) What d'you mean?

GRACE   I'm not a mother. (*Beat.*) It's not me.

DAVINA   Oh, nonsense. You're a fantastic mother.

GRACE   Yeah, right. Don't believe you.

DAVINA   You are! Honestly!

GRACE   Then why do you always tell me what I'm doing wrong?

DAVINA   (*beat*) I don't.

GRACE   Yes, you do. (*Pause.*) You don't like being grandmother, do you? You'd rather be mother.

DAVINA   Oh, Christ, am I just like Nan?

GRACE   (*beat*) No. No, you're not.

    (*Over the baby monitor we hear* MAGGIE *interacting cheerfully with Zoe.*)

DAVINA   I'm sorry. Sometimes, I can't shut up because . . . (*Pause.*) I don't know why. Maybe because I feel guilty. About my own mistakes. I'm trying to . . . make amends somehow . . .

GRACE   (*frowns*) What mistakes?

DAVINA   Nobody really knows what's right and wrong. (*From the baby monitor we hear a silly toy noise.*) What is she doing? Why is she playing with toys? (*Beat.*) You can't be a perfect parent. You just have to be good enough. And you are!

GRACE   (*sarcastic*) Oh, thanks.

DAVINA   It's a compliment.

GRACE   What, that I'm 'good enough'?

DAVINA   Good enough is the best there is, as far as parenting
              goes.

              (*Another silly noise.* DAVINA *frowns at it.*)

GRACE   Whatever. It's just too tough. I didn't realise how
              tough it would be.

DAVINA   You'll be fine. Honestly. Everything will be just fine.

              (DAVINA *puts her arms around* GRACE *who leans into
              her mother. But their hug is interrupted by another
              toy noise.*)

              Why is she playing with fucking toys? Why is she
              stimulating her?

GRACE   I don't care.

DAVINA   Well, I do. (*Checks watch.*) It's late.

              (DAVINA *gets up.*)

Grace   Mum?

              (DAVINA *leaves the room, muttering, followed by*
              GRACE. *More silly toy noises from the baby monitor.*
              BEN *wanders in, beer in hand, and looks around the
              room. He fiddles with the iPod dock. 'Have Yourself
              a Merry Little Christmas' by Judy Garland is heard.
              Further silly noises from the baby monitor, followed
              by the sound of* DAVINA *asking* MAGGIE, *politely,
              what she's doing.* BEN *listens. We hear* GRACE *talking
              lovingly to Zoe while* DAVINA *and* MAGGIE *disagree
              with each other in the background.* GRACE *asks them
              to take it outside.* BEN *switches the baby monitor
              off. He then finds his father's framed photo behind
              some Christmas cards and brings it to the front.
              He contemplates it, then raises his glass in a silent
              toast. Then he sits and listens to the song.*)

              (*Lights and music fade.*)